Mend Your Wings and Fly

Also by Stacey Diaz:

"Fly"

I would love to connect with you via these other avenues... Please reach out!

CONTACT INFORMATION
Stacey Elaine Diaz
Butterflies Fly
PO Box 1394
Vienna, Il 62995

You Tube Channel: Butterflies Fly

Email: diazstacey777@gmail.com

Facebook: Stacey Diaz

https://m.facebook.com/staceyediaz/

https://m.facebook.com/staceycorzine/

Facebook Blog:
https://m.facebook.com/butterfliesflymendyourwings

Instagram:

Butterfliesfly95

Butterflyspeakercoach

Butterfliesfly5k

Bonverabutterfly

Staceyediaz

Linked In:
https://www.linkedin.com/profile/view?id=23410350

Twitter: (@79a085b853e544c):
https://twitter.com/79a085b853e544c?s=09

My blog: https://about.me/butterfliesfly

My wordpress blog: butterfliesflymendyourwingsandfly.com

Mend Your Wings and Fly

Stacey Diaz

Dedication

First and foremost, I am grateful to my whisperer of wisdom, my encourager, my angel, my strength, my best friend, my greatest source of love and the one who has stood by my side through every battle and believed in me my entire life, God.

They are my world, the future of our family legacy, chocolate ice cream mixed with oreos on a hot summer day, running through a field of purple wild flowers free, dancing in the woods in the rain. I am so blessed to be the mom of honest, sensitive, old soul Sierra; caring, inspiring , young spirited Sydney; intuitive, friendly, intelligent Tristan and peaceful, loving and gentle Liam.

They are my fellow butterflies. They are the butterflies in my past and the butterflies today that I have had the privilege of being inspired by. Their love has been instrumental in the healing of my wings and it happened so magically with the gentlest touch of their hearts. Without them, this book might've taken 10 more years to write;)

They are every heart who's ever reached my heart. They are all the hearts I've lost, all the hearts I've been blessed with. They are the countless hearts, you, unlocking the door of your heart to receive what is in mine. I am grateful for each and every one of you.. This book has been written from my imagination and it has been sewn together much like a quilt, inspired from the countless memories, dreams, passions, joys, pains and struggles of a well seasoned life, mine.

XOXO,

Stacey

1

Maria's brown eyes met the blue birds pecking at wooden feeders Michael and Jaden crafted the week before. She relaxed on her white, cotton hammock. The surface of the lake was awakened by the reflection of dogwood trees and green grass. A stocked pond that Michael had built trickled into a flowing waterfall. A few years back, Michael and Maria's dad built a wooden bridge which crossed over the lake into the back yard. A nest tucked into a flower box on the front porch protected a couple of blue eggs. The mother was not in sight. The birds and frogs serenaded Maria's joy filled heart.

Michael walked out wearing a blue, cotton bathrobe. He was blessed with the gift of a Cherokee Indian complexion. His thick, wavy black hair draped over his glistening forehead. His ocean colored eyes enticed hers to take a dip. One of his arms hugged her waist as he handed her a French vanilla latte and pecked her cheek.

"How's my love doing this morning?"

"Good...Thank you, babe."

"Whatcha thinkin' about?"

"Why do you always ask me that, Michael?"

"For the same reason you ask me when we're sittin' in the car on a long trip, honey!"

"Why do I do that?" she thought.

Memories swarmed her mind of how his charismatic ways had them frequently entertained. One time, she came to class and none of the kids showed up. She was perplexed as she searched for the calendar. Michael had convinced the principal to give her the day off so he could take her away for the weekend for their anniversary. When they arrived in Chicago, he tucked a $100 bill under a sleeping woman's hand. He never asked for anything back. There were countless times he had dinner ready before she walked in the house. Occasionally, they picked a movie out together and would leave with his choice. Maria chuckled about his rare moments of being human. Every once in awhile she questioned her own. His good natured ways of charming every person who crossed his path made her want to get better.

"What do ya got planned for today, Maria?"

"Getting dressed, teaching freshman about Queen Elizabeth, eating lunch with a handsome accountant, then home for maybe a bubble bath."

"Someone has a date with my wife! What a lucky man he is! Guess I should stand in line for your next date or meet you in the bubbles tonight."

"I'll put you on my list, honey."

Michael kissed Maria's cheek, jumped in his jeep and drove to the office. Maria sipped her French vanilla latte while checking her social media accounts.

"Time for school Michaela!"

Maria climbed the steep stairs to her daughter's bedroom.

Sunlight peeking through her black curtains illuminated her complexion. Michaela, with almond eyes squinting, slowly arose from her pillow. She wore a frightful expression. A bit of her mopped, naturally curly black hair soaked drool.

"Will you hand me my glasses, Mom?"

"Sure, where are they?"

"On the floor... I think."

"You can barely see and you don't take the best care of these. Look how bent they are?"

"Lay off mom, I fell asleep writing a paper."

"What's for breakfast Mommy?" Jaden yelled as he ran up the stairs.

"How about a pop tart or a pancake to go, Buddy?"

"With a cup of syrup and some apple juice, Mommy?"

"Sure, bud!"

"Don't cook them for too long, because I want them to be soft and fluffy."

"When did you learn how to cook pancakes, Jaden? Let's go downstairs and let your sister get ready for school."

"Whenever you cook them too long, they get hard, Mommy."

Jaden had become a sponge in the kitchen since he had entered kindergarten.

"Nice dress, Michaela. In my days, plaid pants didn't go with flowers?"

"Thanks Mom, I think. I'm hip. I'm cool and I'm making my own style."

"Are you ok Michaela?"

"You know I'm not a morning person Mom and I like sleep these days."

They rode to school in a mutually acceptable and appreciated silence.

"What's that, Michaela?"

"I bet it's an ad.   Turn your windshield wipers on..."

"No, and why are you always ordering me around, Michaela?"

"Chillax! I get it from you, Mom."

"I don't order you around Michaela."

"Just a hint of bossy, Mom. Haaaave I told you how much I love you today?"

Maria pulled to the side of the gravel road and pulled the paper as she got back into the car.

"What does it say, Mommy?"

"Maria,

You have an inner and outer beauty which truly captivates the world. I am the luckiest man in the world. Redeem this coupon for a night of massages and head tingles.

I love you,

Michael."

"Geeez, where does he get this stuff Mom? Does he buy these letters online?"

"From his heart, Michaela. Your father has always had a way with words."

"Oooooh, Mommy." Jaden sighed.

Maria dropped Michaela off and took Jaden to class before arriving to her classroom. The morning went by rather quickly and at the end of class, Mr. Berndino, the phys Ed teacher peeked in.

"Whatcha think about a dance to raise money for Beta Club?"

"Hmm, Mr. Berndino, that sounds like a fabulous idea. Who are you thinking for the chaperones?"

Mr. Berndino gave her a blank stare.

"Ugh, ok, Michael and I will do it if you and Jill will be there."

"I'll talk to Jill."

"Ok, Michael is coming to meet me for lunch if you want to join us?"

"No, you lovebirds go ahead and enjoy yourselves. I have papers to grade."

"Why don't you get those done at home, Berndino?"

"Because my home time is for me and Jill. In fact, I need to get in my car and drive, riiiiight now." Berndino said after he glanced at his watch.

"So tell me what your thoughts are on Queen Elizabeth, class."

In walked Michael balancing a crystal vase of roses.

"Hi class, is it ok if I steal Maria away now? It will give you an extra 15 minutes?"

A simultaneous and cheerful "yes" echoed into the hallway!

Michael and Maria took the jeep to the lake a couple blocks away. Michael reached over to kiss Maria.

Are we going to eat outside Mr. Maxen ?" Maria said as she pulled away.

"How about a little more kissing, Mrs. Maxen?"

"We only have an hour before my next class, honey. How about we walk over to that picnic table?" Maria said grinning.

"Sure babe, I brought you your favorite..."

"Baked mostaccoli?"

"Um...Your other favorite, an Italian beef sandwich with melted provolone. For dessert, rest your eyes upon this chocolate mousse cake with two forks!"

Maria went to grab the cake.

"Uh uh. Italian beef first, a kiss for Michael and then chocolate mousse cake."

"You always make everything so perfect, Michael. How do you always know what to do?"

" I read a lot, baby. You know my mom. She raised a gentleman and I get ideas sent to my digital book."

"Now, I know you did not get last night's fun from a book. That came directly from your imagination, Michael."

"Your happiness is important to me. My gosh, you have the sexiest eyes."

"And your happiness is important to me, Michael."

"How about I wash your back with that little pink, puffy thing tonight?"

"How about you put Jaden to bed and read to him and I will bathe myself, honey? I have to go back to work."

"Well, that was cold, Maria."

Maria grabbed Michael's hand.

"You're right. Remember that time we drove to Virginia and it was midnight and…?"

"Yeeeeesssss, Maria. Tell me more."

"Think about that all day today, Mr. Maxen."

"I will, Mrs. Maxen."

As the day progressed, Maria gradually woke up and before she knew it, it was time to give the kids time to do their homework. The sun's reflection shining her classroom window took a hold of her glowing thoughts. The day seemed to drag on like decades.

"Class, by Monday I want you to write 3 pages about anything you want. "

"Anything? "

"Yes, any ideas, Jacob?"

How about I write about you."

"Wooah… Guess I should be grateful you are thinking about me enough to write about me, or maybe there is a problem?"

"No problems here, Teacher."

"Great, Jacob, I will see you tomorrow."

Maria picked up Michaela and Jaden and they arrived home.

Maria walked in to the sound of the dryer tumbling and the smell of dryer sheets.

"Hey honey...How lucky am I to come home to my man doing the job I hate the most. You are such a gift. "

"Thank you for being the most incredible wife a man could ask for."

Michael wrapped his arms around her hips and pecked her on the cheek.

"What are you buttering me up for, Michael?"

"Me, butter you up? Never, I'm innocent, Mrs. Maxen."

"Whenever those eyes look at me in that way it's usually because you want something. The last time this happened, we went to the Bahamas, listened to a speech for an hour and bought a time share we still don't use. I know you want something."

"Well, as a matter of fact, how about a boat, baby?"

"Michael, we have a house, we have cars and you know boats are the worst investment. They will suck the money out of our pockets."

"I know, but they're so much fun," squealed Michael. "Picture it. You, me, alone, it's sunset, no kids, at the lake, catfish fishing and maybe a little swimming."

"You aren't talking about one of those really expensive house boats that we have to make payments on are you, Michael?"

"Nope, this one is used and it's a beaut., baby."

"Don't you think it's kind of selfish to be thinking about a boat when my birthday is coming up?"

"Have I ever failed you on your birthday?"

"Never baby... Late every once in awhile but never a failure."

"Then why do you always get so weird on your birthday?"

"You know when I was growing up my birthdays were never important and I get really uncomfortable wondering about it all. How much do you want?"

"$500 buckaroonis will buy it and I have to go to Chicago next week to pick it up."

"On my birthday?!"

"Nope, the day before. You want to come with me babe?"

"Picking up a boat, YOUR boat, is not my idea of how I would like to spend my birthday!"

"We can go to that Greek restaurant you love so much and split a beef roll, honey?"

"Ooh...now Im sold! Not that you care or understand how I feel!"

"Oh, I know how you feel! You always make sure I know how you feel!"

"Wait, honey, where are you going?"

"To do some cyber shopping. Looks like if you are spending $500, I have a grand birthday gift to buy and I love black diamonds."

"Whatever you want sweetie!"

Maria got really excited when she searched online for a picture of a sparkling ½ carat diamond with amazing clarity from an online wholesaler.

"Happy Birthday to me. This baby will be on this finger. Yee hah!" Maria said.

She pulled out her gently used credit card, and like a thief, guilt swooped in and stole her temporary smile.

Whenever they argued, she found herself in deep mind paralysis for hours wishing she could go back in time and eliminate the built up tension. She would much rather starve the deep cries from her own soul to feed her love and passion to his heart.

Jaden walked in the sunroom.

"Hey Mommy. Would you please read me a really long bedtime story?"

"If you give me a great big hug and a kiss and come sit on my lap, Buddy."

They sat for awhile reading and into the sunroom walked Michael.

"Hey Daddy!"

"Hey Buddy, whatcha doing?"

"Mommy's reading me a story. Want to sit with us?"

"Sure Buddy. Why don't you head in the bathroom and Mommy will be there in a little bit?"

Michael walked up to Maria

"Honey, if you don't want me to get the boat I won't, I just thought..."

Maria interrupted Michael, "No, I want you to get it. I love you and I want you to be happy Baby."

Looking into Maria's soul, Michael pulled her chin in close to his and kissed her like he did when they were 22. How about you meet me in a fantasy tonight for a warm bubble bath and some wine?"

"Maybe, Mr. Maxen. It depends."

"On what, Mrs. Maxen?"

"Hmmm...Entice me."

She felt his warm breath tickle her ear, radiating a fire of passion racing down the side of her neck.

"You so have me at your service, Sir…30 minutes and I'll be back."

Michael laid on the couch mesmerized, watching his beautiful, Italian love walk out of the room.

"I'll be waiting for you…"

Maria left to give Jaden a bath..

As the end of the night drew close, Maria walked into the dark bedroom. A faint light glimmer shone from around the corner. She followed the dancing, yellow lights and shadows around the garden tub. Bubbles blanketed Michael's hairy chest.

"How's about you get in here with your baby?"

"Hmmm, are you tempting me?"

Maria felt an electrical jolt inside her stomach and Michael guided her chin toward his, gently reacquainting his lips with hers. He took her foot in his hands, gliding across the soap suds with her pink puff.

Maria gently grabbed for Michael's hand as he giddily climbed out of the garden tub.

"Where are you going handsome?"

"I'll be boooock in un memento."

Michael raced to the laundry room, pulling her fuzzy, white cotton robe.

"Are you ready to get out beautiful?"

"Yes, I am."

Michael wrapped her toasty robe around Marias body as hot tingles chased her shivers away. Without a word, Maria followed him to their comfortable nest. Their reflection on the wall invited moonlight for a dance, while entertaining darkness. A gentle wind tousled the curtains across the soft white bear rug. The evening glided in yet disappeared so swiftly. Michael tickled her feet, awakening the rest of her body.

"Good morning," he whispered into her ear as his breath sent goosebumps speeding down the surface of her back."

"Let's stay in bed all day, Baby cakes."

"Sounds nice, but what do we do about work, Michael?"

"Let's take off today and I'll take the kids to school. I'll return with a few good movies...aaaand we can recreate last night."

You often paint such beautiful visions for me to dream about my love, but you know, the only time I ever take off is if there is a snow day."

"Oh yes," said Michael. I remember that time we hung out in the hot tub and watched the snowfall. You looked so cute with snowflakes stuck in your pony tail and your bright red nose. Do you remember that?"

"Yes, it was fun,"

Smiling, Maria ripped off the satin covers and slowly climbed out of their king size bed. Michael gently pulled her back for a kiss before the busyness of the day distracted each of them from their mush.

Jaden knocked at the door and Maria opened it.

"Let me guess Jaden. Yooooou're hungry?"

"What do you want to eat buddy?"

"Pizza!"

"Pizza, Jaden…I have no pizza."

"Fine. A waffle, Mommy."

"Would you like a waffle, Michael?"

"No, I have to go in early today."

Maria went downstairs and began beating the eggs in coffee mugs like she had watched online the other day. Jaden tried one bite and spit it out.

"You don't like it Jaden?"

"Mommy, these don't take like the eggs you normally make?"

Maria tried a bite and almost spit it out herself.

"How are the waffles? I made them with my new waffle iron."

"The waffles are good, Mommy."

Michael kissed Maria and left. When he arrived to the parking lot, he called to reserve a room at a high end hotel downtown and made reservations at one of Chicago's finest Italian restaurants' downtown. He bought some tickets to see a musical.

"I'm the man, I'm her man, and now to the jewelry store."

"How about this piece, sir?"

"Nah, she is much more about simplicity yet elegance,"

"How about this one, Mr. Maxen?"

"Perfect."

Meanwhile, Maria dropped the kids off at school and arrived to her class

"Hi, Mrs. Maxen,"

"Hi Lola, how are you sweetheart?"

"Good, Mrs. Maxen!"

"I love that outfit. You always put so much of your personality into your outfits. You remind me of Michaela when she was younger."

"Thank you, Mrs. Maxen."

"The last time we talked, your sister was having trouble with common core math. How is it going for her now sweetheart?"

"Not good. My mom, dad and I tried to help her with her homework, but I don't think any of our answers are right. Mom took her paper, read it and started figuring out the answers really quickly and I told her she may have the right answer but she was doing it all wrong. Then my dad tried to figure out the answer. He pretended like he had a phone call and said mom would have to do it."

"How did you know your dad pretended like he got a phone call? Maria chuckled.

"'Cause his phone normally makes a loud noise when it vibrates."

"Who finally helped her?"

"My sister Lynn, Mrs. Maxen."

"Did she do it right?"

"Yes, we don't trust mom and dad with common core math."

"I think common core is hard for moms and dads these days because it requires an entirely different way of thinking."

"Well, at least Lynn can help me with it."

"I don't mind to help you too. In fact, tell your parent's I would be glad to tutor them."

"Ok, Mrs. Maxen, I will."

Maria was approached by another student, Alan.

"Hi, Mrs. Maxen."

"Hi Alan! How are you Buddy?"

"Doing great!"

"How are you doing with your report on "King James?""

"I'll have it done really soon Mrs. Maxen."

"How are you getting it done so quickly?"

"I don't know, I write my structure and then build it from there."

"Hmmm...A few of my students are having trouble, but you are coming along quite smoothly. Good for you Alan!"

"Thank you Mrs. Maxen. Ask me about History and that's a whole 'nother ball game. I can't stay awake in that class no matter how hard I try. "

"You know, history was not my best classes either, well... until the last few years anyway."

"What makes you like it now at your age?"

"Hey, hey on the age sir. I enjoy learning about the leaders in history, the battles they fought, who they were, what they stand for and what attributed to their character."

"That's deep Mrs. Maxen."

"I love to learn. Never stop growing and learning, Alan."

"Ok, Mrs.. Maxen."

The clock hand moved at lightning speed. Maria gathered her papers to grade, met Jaden and Michaela and it was time to head home.

"What's for dinner, Mom?"

"Any ideas, Michaela?"

"How about spaghetti like grandmas?"

"Ok."

"Can we go get some onion rings, Mommy?"

"No, Jaden, we are going to make dinner tonight.

"But, Mommy."

"No Mommy's Jaden, we are eating at home."

Maria walked in to see Michael, hiding something on the computer and had beaten them home. It struck her a little odd since she was used to him coming home a few hours later.

"Whatcha home so early for, Michael?"

"I finished with a client early, and thought I would come home to see my amazing family. Is that ok?"

"Sure babe, you know me and always asking questions."

"Yes, I do, now what are we doing for dinner?

"Spaghetti."

"What's for dessert? You?"

"Dishes, Michael, dishes."

"Well, then I guess I will head out and burn some leaves and build us a fire for later."

After dinner, everyone ventured out to the swing. The aroma of burning leaves filled the air.

"Who wants a s'more?"

"I do, Mommy."

Maria pulled out a couple of graham crackers, added a marveloulsy melting chocolate bar and Michael handed her a marshmallow.

"Here you go Buddy,"

"Yumm."

The melting chocolate mixing with marshmallow coated his red cheeks.

"Do you know what firemen do when they go to a fire Daddy?"

"What do they do, Buddy?"

"They slide down a long pole."

"Yes, they do Buddy. Did you have a good trip to the fire station?"

"Yeah I did, Daddy."

Who's ready for a bed time story?"

"I am, Daddy."

With speed in her step, Maria headed to her bedroom to color and watch TV.

"Are we going to church tomorrow, my lovely wife?"

"I would really like to, Michael."

Getting ready for church posed it's challenges from time to time at the Maxen house. Church was a part of Maria's life since she was a little girl. As a little girl, she remembered sitting in Sunday school with her grandma and doing devotions. She often felt chills and moved to tears from the Holy Spirit when listening to church songs. She often felt clarity and purity when listening to God's whispers.

"I am meeting with a group of men tonight, Maria."

"Ok, when will you be home?"

"Always questions baby. In about an hour."

"I don't know why this is a surprise to you, Michael. Everyone in my family asks questions."

"I love you baby."

"I love you too Michael."

The evening passed and Michael came home.

"How was group?"

"A little concerning."

"How so?"

Joe mentioned he had an affair."

"What? How is Renae doing about this?"

"Of course she is flipping mad, but they are working on making it work."

"Who did he cheat on her with?"

"Kristy."

"That blonde bimbo that was all over Joe when we went on that spiritual retreat?"

"Let's not call anyone names, Maria."

"Ok, ok, said Maria. It is so shocking, and I feel sorry for Renae. I hope you don't side with him and his actions."

"No, I don't side with him and his actions but I'm also not going to judge my friend."

The week passed by rather quickly and Michael and Maria made their way to Chicago.

"Want a latte birthday girl?"

"No."

"Well, that sounded a little better then a grunt, Maria"

The first couple of hours of the trip they quietly listened to classical music. When Michael saw Maria smile at him, it was his cue to speak to her.

"Since it's your birthday, how about you decide on lunch?"

"Anywhere with steak and potatoes and chocolate mousse pie."

Michael did an online search for restaurants.

"Guess what baby? Jeffrey's steaks will be our 2500th little dive restaurant we have eaten at."

They both fell in love with finding treasures of old authentic and unpopular places early on in their dating.

"What are our names and what is our story?

"Let's be wanderers, Michael."

"Where are we headed, Maria?"

"Hooooow's about Washington, Baby?"

"How many?" asked the hostess.

"2."

"Your name?"

"Talidagopolis."

"It'll be about 30 minutes, sir."

"Awesome. Thank you, Mam."

"Talidagopolis? Really? Where did you come up with that name?"

"It's fun to say isn't it, Maria. Say it baby, say it."

"Talidagopolis. You are funny, Michael, always making me laugh!"

"Taleeeedag o pole is," stumbled the waiter.

"That's us."

The waiter seated them at a table.

"Could we get a booth?"

"Sure, sir."

Maria sat down and Michael sat next to her.

"Where are we going to pick up this boat, Mr Maxen?"

"Chicago."

"I get Chicago Michael, I just meant which part."

"Remember that one time we stayed at the Sheraton?"

"The Sheraton, that sounds really nice, Michael. Whatcha gonna order my sexy wanderer?"

"I'm going for the steak sandwich, how about you babe?"

"That sounds good to me."

They ordered their steak sandwiches, ate and mindlessly chatted before leaving. After 5 hours of driving, they finally arrived to the Sheraton.

"Babe, you wait in the car and I will go check us in." Michael Giddily said.

"Ok, babe."

"Hi, I'm Michael Maxen and I have a special reservation. "

"Yes, Mr. Maxen, I see you had us order some surprises to accommodate your wife's birthday?"

"Yes, I trust that everything was done?"

"Yes, Mr. Maxen."

Michael pulled out a $100 bill and tipped him.

"Mr. Maxen, we don't do tips here."

"It's ok, I do."

Michael ran out to the car yelling, "I love Maria Maxen!"

Marias face turned red and the people passing by gave them a smile.

Upon reaching their room, Maria's big eyes caught the shiny silver "Happy Birthday" balloons sitting on the bed with Godiva Carmel chocolates. Maria ran to the card and opened it up. It read, "roses are red, violets are blue, and you thought we were buying a boat but this is really all about you! Happy Birthday!"

"What a jerk. You let me believe it was about you?"

"You want to go home?"

"No, I love you so much, Mr. Maxen."

Maria got on her tippy toes to kiss him.

"What are we doing?"

"I can't tell you everything, or it will ruin all the fun, baby."

"First stop is dinner."

"Dinner, I didn't bring dress clothes so hopefully we are not going anywhere too fancy."

"That's ok, my love, I brought you a dress."

"Which one?"

"Your black sexy strapless one."

"Hmm... sounds like you picked that for your own personal gain."

"Selfish, you caught me. Now, put this on too."

Michael handed Maria a small black box. When she opened it there were black diamond hoop earrings in them.

"Wooooow, Michael! How beautiful! Thank you! I am such a lucky woman."

"Did you say I will get lucky, Mrs. Maxen?"

"If you are lucky, hot stuff!"

"I love the way my baby flirts with me."

"Are you going to get in the shower, baby?"

"I am. Then maybe you can help me get into that sexy black dress?"

"You know I am here to help dress you, brush your hair…Undress you."

Michael walked into the bathroom and caught Marias eyes before he walked to the sink to shave.

"Whatcha doing?" Maria asked.

"Shaving,"

"You know babe, there is a mirror that won't fog up in the room."

"Really? Oh my, I didn't see it."

The shower turned off. Michael grabbed a towel and handed it to Maria.

"I am so spoiled, Michael."

"You deserve it, babe, you put up with me."

Maria put her dress on and Michael zipped it while stealing a kiss from the nape of her neck. She took her time diligently applying her make up.

"Should I put my hair in an updo?"

"Updo and I will help you unravel it tonight. Which jeans should I wear?"

"They are both the same, Michael."

"Nope, they're different, but they look the same."

It took Maria a minute to get what he was trying to say.

"I pick these, handsome."

"These are the jeans I wore the night we went to the races."

"Oh, I remember that night...When mud flew into the crowd and hit me, in the face. Why do these things always happen to me?"

"Yes, that was fun and you were sexy with mud all in your pony tail...You are beautiful and that's your cross to bear, honey."

"What is your cross to bare and what is your fascination with ponytails?"

"My cross to bare is all the questions I have to answer and I love how cute you are modeling a bouncy and carefree pony tail."

"Very funny. Are you making fun of me, Mr. Maxen?"

"Never, there is an awesome piano bar down the road."

"How did you hear about it?"

"I have my connections, Maria Maxen."

The reflection of the fluorescent lights scattered across the floor.

"What do you want to talk about, Maria?"

"You, baaaaby."

"What about muah?"

"You have just outdone yourself and I want you to know I really appreciate all of your efforts, babe."

"You deserve it and I love you too."

They enjoyed many brief moments of soul filled connecting... Maria took in and savored every moment of making such a beautiful memory. After Dinner, they made their way into the city. Michael knew how much Maria loved boat rides. She thought about how fun it would be to bring Jaden and Michaela.

"Now where are we going?" Asked Maria

"Well, I didn't lie completely, the money was for a boat...Well, an evening boat ride."

"What a sweet idea, Michael. What kind of boat ride?"

"A very slow ride down lake Michigan."

Maria's eyes opened wide in surprise as they approached the boat lit with 100s of candles. Classical music softly played in the background.

"May I have this dance, beautiful?

"Why of course Mr. Maxen."

Time stood at attention as their hearts danced to the music. Maria could have lived in this moment forever. After a little time passed, they found a bench and watched the full bright moon illuminate the lake water. Michael pulled out a blanket from his backpack and draped it over Marias lap, tucking the edges under her legs.

"Guess what else I brought, sweetheart."

"Dessert?" Maria softly said.

"Deeesseeert is tonight at the hotel." Michael chuckled.

"Hmm, Mr. Maxen."

Michael pulled out her bright pink and purple fuzzy socks.

"You spoil me, Michael. You really spoil me."

This particular moment was put on pause when Maria's phone rang.

"What are you doing Mommy?"

"On a boat with Daddy."

"A boat? Are you having fun, Mommy?"

"Yes, Jaden, how about I take some pictures for you? Are you having fun with Angelia?"

"Yes Mommy, but I miss you and Daddy.. When will you be home?"

"In a couple of days, Buddy. What have you guys been up to?"

"We went to the fall fair today and walked around and played outside."

"Did you ride any rides Jaden?"

"Yes, I rode the motorcycles and played the duck game."

"Did you win any prizes?"

"Yes, a little stuffed duck, Mommy."

"Good for you Buddy! How's your sister doing?"

"She is good."

"How is Daddy doing?"

"He is doing good sweetie. Do you want to talk to him?"

"Yes, Mommy."

"Hi Buddy! How are you?"

"Good, I drew you a picture, Daddy."

"What did you draw Buddy?"

"A picture of our family- you, Mommy, me, Michaela and Squirt."

"I can't wait to see it, Buddy."

"Daddy, can we go fishing when you come home?"

"That is a great idea, Buddy."

"Gotta go Daddy, Angelia said dinner is ready. I love you! Tell Mommy bye and I love her too."

"Ok, I will Buddy."

"Now, where were we beautiful?" Asked Michael.

"We were watching the moonlight glisten off the silver colored lake water and you were about to twirl me around and wrap your arms around me, and..."

Michael pulled out his black fuzzy socks, "We are going to race across the dance floor in our socks. Ready. Set. Go!"

They raced across the dance floor a few times before Michael grabbed Maria's hand and whisked her away to dance under the moonlight. After awhile, the captain came out to tell them it was time to get off at the Pier. They exited off the boat to hear jazz music playing.

"Let's sit here and keep this lonesome bench company." Michael said.

The explosion of fireworks drowned out the music. Michael took her hand and slipped a ring on her finger.

"What is this?"

"It's a promise I will always be right there."

"There you go again, Michael, just another reason to touch my chest."

"The sole reason I married you, Mrs. Maxen."

"You know that's a lie. You married me for my double jointed fingers."

"Got me aaaaaaall figured out, Mr. Maxen."

Maria smiled. She thought about how many times her coworkers looked up in anticipation when the truck delivering flowers would pull into the school district parking lot. It later turned to envy as they watched the trail of red pass them in slow motion arriving to Maria's classroom. She recalled the millionth time Jaden would ask him to read the torn book about turtles and cars and his response was always, "of course Buddy." His ears always seemed open whenever she needed to talk. Whenever he grabbed her hand, she still felt the warm fuzzies.

And then…As they began their walk, the rain was feeling a little left out and joined their party.

"My hair!" yelled Maria.

Michael chuckled.

Michael's steps resembled a slow and timeless dance, splashing in as many puddles as he could. Maria began a slow jog and heard a mischievous laugh come from her best friend. He reached for her hand, gently pulled her into his arms, wiped away her wet hair and kissed her rosy cheek…

Maria wondered if these moments would ever disappear. When her hair was its most natural color of gray, would he still look deep within her soul with passion and ask her heart to come out and play?

They made it to their room where an Italian crème birthday cake with candles and two forks, along with an envelope rested on the bed. At the end of the trail of white and pink rose petals were two doves folded out of washcloths. The Jacuzzi was waiting to swallow the both of them into its hot raging bubbles. Michael began to pour her a glass of chilled bubbling champagne.

"Tickets to see my favorite musical? Wow! Awe baby, I am so excited! Wait…You are going to sit through a musical with me?"

"Of course."

"You did so much more than I ever expected. Thank you! I am so lucky and I love you so much!"

"I love you too. Happy Birthday Baby!"

"Are we ready for some hot tub fun?"

"Yes mam! How about a glass of wine?"

The effort and thought Michael put into making Maria's birthday special made her heart pitter patter aggressively and put her in the mood to be his servant. You can't get much better than this she thought, 13 years of a loving marriage. Her more tightly wound personality seemed to balance his open free spirit. All that separated them from unlocking their souls was the steam from the bubbling hot tub. He grabbed her chin and bit her lip savoring every piece of her as if it was his very first time.

The morning came back so swiftly. Room service delivered scrambled eggs with cheese, Texas style French Toast and chocolate covered strawberries adorned the antique gold rimmed plates. Maria reached for a strawberry teasing Michael with it. Michael growled, shook his head, and then took a bite of it.

"What are we going to do today, Mr. Maxen?"

"How about we stay in bed all day and we can play hide and eat the chocolate covered fruit?"

"Are you sure about that, Michael?"

"No, we can't stay in bed all day or how about half a day? Then we can go for a walk on the Pier before we head to the musical."

"Sounds relaxing and heavenly, babe."

Michael strategically placed a strawberry on Maria's belly button and slipped under the sheets. Maria giggled. He bit into it as he offered Maria a bite. As she swallowed the final bite, they wrestled around before it was time for Maria to get ready.

They left for the musical. The wind was whispering future dreams of hope into Maria's ears. They could see the season's change in the tree's changing colors. The lake waves soothed Maria's anticipation of the future. Holding hands, they walked the Pier before making it to the musical with a few minutes to spare.

"You know Michael, Ever since I was a little girl, I have loved watching musicals. I used to dream of getting up on stage and singing my heart out. Time has moved so fast and after slipping away for a few years you have inspired a few back to life. There's such a passionate and exciting feeling at the thought. I love you babe!"

"I love you too sweetie!"

After the musical, they walked back to the hotel and made the most of their snuggling time before it was time to venture back to the kids.

"Let's call em!" Michael exclaimed.

"Hey, Angelia! Can we talk to the kids?"

"Sure, which one?"

"Whichever one wants to talk to their dad."

"Hi Dad!" Exclaimed Michaela.

"Daaaaad...Are you too old to call me Daddy?"

"Yeah, Dad."

"Well, we miss you guys! What's Jaden doing?"

"Playing cars. Would you like to talk to him?"

"Yes, I'm still his Daddy, haaa!" Laughed Michael.

"Ok, Daddy, I love you. Here's Jaden."

"I love you too Michaela!"

"Hey champ! How's it going?"

"Great, we've been watching movies all day, and we baked a cake for Mommy!"

"What kind?"

"We made her some chocolate cake and birthday cards. Then we went to Clarissa's grandma's house and picked wild flowers for her hair."

"That's awesome, have you gotten to throw the football around?"

"A little bit."

"You sound sad Buddy, what's wrong?"

"I miss you and Mommy, Daddy."

"We miss you too Buddy, we'll be home in 5 hours."

"Ok, then will you play soccer with me?"

"Absolutely, Bud!"

Michael and Jaden hung up.

"They didn't want to talk to their mommy?"

"Nope."

"Do they have something up their sleeve?" asked Maria.

"I'm sworn to secrecy. Let's just throw away the leftover cake."

They arrived back to town and headed to Angelia's house. Maria's eyes lit up to purple, red and blue balloons. Michaela brought over a chocolate cake with chocolate frosting. They had written, "Happy Birthday," in red and blue letters. The house smelled of Filet mignon, Marias favorite. Angelia was holding a package.

"What is it Angelia?"

"Open it, Biatch!"

"Gloves...how practical. Nothing like a best friend who knows you like to keep your hands warm."

"Put them on."

Maria put them on and felt something small and metal pricking at her finger. She pulled the metal out and there was a ring with 3 birthstones in it.

"Wooow, Angelia, this was too much, thank you."

"Nope, you're my best friend and you're worth it."

"Wow guys, thank you."

"Your welcome, Mommy."

"So...let's talk Brody, my man. Shark fishing in Florida in 4 weeks?"

"This is why I love you man!"

"Are the ladies coming with?" Asked Brody.

"Sharks, naaaah. We'll bathe on the beach with the kids while you boys go play."

"Don't say we didn't invite you, ladies!" Exclaimed Michael.

"Picture it Angelia. You, me, tropical drinks and our own personal waiter?"

"I do believe we are the winners here. I can't wait, Angelia."

As time raced by, they headed home to tuck the kids in.

"What do you guys think about heading to the lake and going fishing tomorrow?"

"Sounds fun, Daddy!" said Jaden.

"Personally I would prefer to sleep in, Dad."

"Just one more time, Michaela, just one more time before you are wearing a cap and gown and heading to college."

"Dad, I'm a freshman. We still have quite a bit of time left and enough to get tons of rest."

"I hear you baby girl."

They woke up while it was still dark and drove to the lake. The fog was pretty thick, but, they caught the sun revealing itself from below the green hills. The meadows were hungry for admiration and attention. The crows and and crickets sang a duet. The boat motor purred and little fish splashes of danced to the rhythm of the morning.

"You going to bait your own hook, Michaela?"

"I don't want to fish, DADDY!"

"Why not? You have been fishing with me since you were a little girl."

"Don't get frantic, Daddy, I just want to sleep."

"How on earth can you sleep inside that intertube?"

"It's comfortable for me, Dad."

"Guess it's you and me Jaden."

"Ok, Daddy."

Jaden glowed with pride when he caught a catfish half his size.

"Here...Let me get my selfie stick Jaden. We can measure it and then take a picture of you with it."

"Ok, Mommy."

As the sun began to set, they breezed past the changing leaves. The hands on Michael's watch turned faster than ever before and it was time to get off the water and head home. Nothing would stop their tradition of heading to Tandy's Ice Cream Shop for some chocolate, sprinkle covered cones.

"Who wants a chocolate dipped sprinkled cone?"

No one answered. Michael looked around the car and everyone was sleeping. I guess I'm eating a chocolate dipped sprinkle cone. While listening to some 80s rock, Michael finished his cone before anyone woke up. He stopped at the gas station, got rid of any evidence ice cream was eaten and headed home. They finally arrived home safe and Michael sat down on his brown leather chair next to the overflowing book shelf. Jaden followed and found his place on the stool in front of him with his own book, mimicking his dad's every movement.

"What was your favorite part of today, Jaden?"

"Catching my first catfish Mommy. How about yours?"

"Watching you catch catfish sweetie!"

"Are you ready for bed Jaden?"

"10 more minutes, Mommy, pleeeease?"

"How about we put on a movie in your room Jaden?"

"Ok, Mommy."

Maria walked into Jaden's dark blue room with his fire truck bed and saw Michaela curled up much like she was on the intertube in the boat. Maria's heart smiled and radiated warmth.

"Now Jaden, after that book, it's time for bed."

"How do you make yourself fit Michaela?"

"Flexibility Mom!"

Maria walked back to her bedroom where Michael was working on his lap top and crawled under his comforter. He immediately put his lap top to the side and she laid her head on his soft hairy chest as he tousled her hair around. She loved the feeling of head tingles.

"We are so blessed, baby."

"Yes, yes we are."

Michael kissed her forehead.

"Wait, wait, I'll beeeee right back!"

Within a few minutes, Michael had returned with a gold trimmed white antique plate filled with fresh fruit."

"What are you doing, Michael?"

"Feeding my beautiful wife. Now close your eyes."

"Why, Michael?"

"Why must you ask so many questions, Woman?"

"That is one of the things you fell in love with, remember, my hunger to learn?"

"Yes, yes, but after so many years...are you going to close those beautiful, sexy brown eyes now?"

"Yes, baby."

"Let's play "Guess that fruit."

"Ok, Michael."

"A pineapple."

"That wins you a kiss on the lips from your hot husband."

"Maria climbed on his lap, looked into his innocent eyes and made the moment unforgettable. She then quickly went to her side of the bed."

Michael gave her the next fruit

"Grape."

"That wins you a 2 minute shoulder massage from your amazing husband."

"Niiiiiice, Michael. I like this game."

Maria rolled over on her stomach. Michael massaged her shoulders ending with a soft and gentle kiss at the nape of her neck.

"Chocolate covered strawberry."

"You got it baby! Now that wins me a massage and a free 5 minutes of tickling you."

Michael began to tickle her and the world could hear her echoing laugh.

"Stop, Michael!"

Magnetism drew the two of them close as he wiped a tear from her eye. They became completely entangled into one another's spirits. In the morning, the sun shone into the bedroom and Maria woke up with a nauseous feeling in her stomach as she caught a glimpse of their first snow fall of the year.

She tip toed to the porch covered in 3 inches of snow after making herself a cup of coffee. As she tripped she saw a dead crow lying in front of the door.

"Hey baby, would you please come get this dead bird off my porch?"

"Sure…You know I'm at home and you don't have to text me."

"Yes and what are you trying to say?"

"Well, I would love to hear your voice."

"Michael, you hear my voice every single day. Will you please come get this dead bird off the porch?"

Michael came out to check the lifeless bird with a large glove and took it to the woods behind their house.

"I have a feeling someone is going to die, Michael."

"I think your imagination is playing tricks on you again, baby."

"I'm not crazy, Michael."

"I know this baby, but you know I'm not superstitious or suspicious like you are. What you say becomes your reality."

"What do you mean suspicious, Michael?"

"Well, you have to admit, you do ask a lot of questions, Maria.

"I told you I ask a lot of questions because I'm a learner but think whatever you want."

Michael went to kiss her on her cheek and she pushed him away with a look of irritation.

"Awe, baby, I love you, you are sooo cute."

"I'm going to get into the shower and get ready for work. Would you mind to go get Jaden ready?"

"Of course I don't mind. Although, I would much rather be washing your long black hair in a hot steamed shower."

"Maybe next time."

"Jaden, it's time to get up for school, Buddy!"

"Already awake, Daddy! I just have to put my shoes on."

Maria began to daydream about her "secret powers" and appreciated the years of solid trust she and Michael had built. She wondered how the rest of the world could comprehend the gift she sometimes saw as a plague. The only women who understood were the women in her family. She rarely understood it herself, often times walking it to a door in her mind labeled irrational. And when one of her premonitions came true, "ugh" would take a walk outside the door. On the way home, Maria did not feel like cooking so she and the kids grabbed some Chinese takeout from the restaurant down the road. As she pulled into the driveway, she noticed that Michaels car had not made it home yet. She remembered he had a meeting til 7pm. She saw 7:30 roll over on the digital clock and Michael did not show up. Then, 8:00 pm rolled around and Maria thought she better call him.

"Where is he?" she thought hearing his congenial "You have reached Michael Maxen…" after she called to check on him.

At 9pm, Maria's mind began to flood with waves of doubt and worry as she put Jaden to bed and said goodnight to Michaela.

"Is Daddy home yet?"

"No, I am sure he will be home soon, Michaela."

"I'm getting worried, Mom."

"I'm a little worried too, but I am pretty sure no news is good news, sweetie."

At 9:30pm, Maria's stomach sank when she answered her phone.

"Hello."

"Hi, may I speak to Michael Maxen's wife?

"This is her."

A feeling of intense fear exploded out of Maria's stomach.

"Hi, Mrs. Maxen, this is Hope Memorial Hospital and I regret to inform you that your husband, Michael Maxen has been in a terrible car accident."

"Is he ok, mam?"

"I think it is best we don't talk about his condition over the phone, Mrs. Maxen."

Flashbacks of Christmas with the kids swarmed her worried mind. She thought about their last conversation and knew she needed to make it up to him, hug him and tell him how much she loved him.

"Angelia, can you come stay with the kids? Michael has been in a terrible car accident?"

"Of course, but you aren't going by yourself. Brody and I will bring the kids and I will go with you. I'll drive, Maria."

Angelia nudged Maria to the passenger door. As they passed by a t intersection, Maria caught the glimpse of what resembled Michael's Jeep.

"This all has to be some sort of mistake or misunderstanding." she thought.

Reality began to fill her hopeful heart as she recognized the white family stickers on the trunk that he and Jaden had proudly put on a few weeks before.

Maria and Angelia walked up to the admittance desk of the emergency room.

"I am here to see Michael Maxen."

"Yes, Mam. Let me get the nurse you need to speak to."

The nurse walked out.

"Maria, come sit down. We tried to save your husband but the trauma to his brain and lungs were too great for his body to take. Unfortunately, Michael passed away upon arrival to the hospital."

Maria's eyes met her mind with denial. A gaping sinkhole began to open in her heart and Angelia grabbed a hold of her tightly as she screamed and cried out "Michael!"

"Mam, would you like to come say goodbye and identify him? You will have a couple of hours before we have to take him out of the room."

"Really...let me get this straight...the love of my life just passed away, and no I'm sorry? You want to make sure I'm out in a couple of hours?"

"Yes mam, I am so very sorry."

"Take me to my husband,"

"Do you want me to go with, Maria?" Asked Angelia.

"Yeah."

Maria continued choking back tears before finally entering the room. Michael's lifeless body looked nothing like it did the morning he left her.

"This can't be real."

She hugged Angelia as their eyes were pouring tears. She noticed the tattoo on his ring finger they got on their honeymoon. It had her initials and "forever hers" beneath his white gold plated wedding band. Maria felt the most horrific pain begin to gnaw in the middle of her heart. She climbed on top of the bed and laid next to him where her head found comfort on his chest. She grasped him tightly yearning to feel his warmth and hid arms reach back for hers.

"It's him, Angelia, it's him.."

"Mam, you can take as long as a couple of hours, but we will need to know where to take him. Maria sat there frozen and in shock and called her parents to come meet them. Nothing seemed real. Maria convinced herself she must have been one of his many practical jokes that just went too far. Michael was just alive in the morning.

"Michael baby, tell me this is all a joke."

She tightly gripped his hand.

"Come on baby, hold my hand."

When her parents walked in, they embraced her.

"Can you please call his parents and the funeral home, Mom?"

"Sure, sweetie."

She held his hand the last couple of hours, which seemed like minutes, before the funeral home finally came to pick him up. Marias mom peeled Maria away from Michael as they prepared to take him to the funeral home. Tears streamed down her mascara stained face.

"Come on baby."

"I don't want to leave him, Mom."

Her mom brushed her hair to the side.

"You have to now, Sweetie."

"Have you told Brody, Angelia?"

"No, Michael is his best friend, we have to tell him in person."

"I will drive you back Angelia, but I think Maria needs a little time before going in and telling the kids."

"We'll grab some sandwiches and come back."

"Ok."

"What is going on Angelia?" asked Brody as she walked in.

Angelia motioned Brody to the bathroom where she told him the news. He got on his knees and hugged Angelia's legs as he repeated, "This can't be true."

Maria's eyes had zoned out into a distant place while her dad pulled through the drive thru to grab some breakfast sandwiches.

"What would you like to eat, Maria?"

"Not hungry, Dad." Maria said solemnly.

"I will order you something and you can eat it later babe."

"Ok, Dad." Maria cried.

"I am going to drive around a little bit," Maria said as they pulled up to the house.

"Are you sure you can drive ok?"

"Yeah Dad, really, I will be ok."

"Call us if you need anything, Maria. We will wait for your call."

"I just need to process this all. I will call you tomorrow." Maria said hugging each of her parents goodbye.

Butterflies flew like mad in the pit of her stomach. Surely the man she saw was not the man who played tennis with her during a thunderstorm, stopped the car dancing with her to the moonlight during the darkest nights, or magically made her head tingle almost every time that routine pain from each days stressors attacked her mind. The aroma of her favorite coffee still filled her car from the last time he touched her nose and kissed her forehead with his gentleness. She could barely swallow the chunks of her breakfast. The pictures he made gave her an unbelievably strong stabbing pain in the center of her chest. Her throat felt the pressure of swallowing every last bit of the news she just heard.

Both sides of the road were covered in snow and an invisible and angelic force must have taken complete control of her drive. As she approached their home, they spent most of their early married years, tears rolled down her already painted black rosy cheeks.   How would she break the news to the kids? Who was going to dress up like Santa and hand out Christmas presents or put the Christmas lights up? Who would read to Michael?

Michaela and Jaden were standing at the front door with anticipation.

"Where is Daddy?" asked Jaden.

"I have some very bad news, guys…"

"What, Mommy?"

"Daddy went to heaven last night.""

"What? This can't be real Mom! This is a sick joke!" exclaimed Michaela.

"They held each other tightly with tears streaming into puddles on the floor."

The next day Maria and Michael's parents met her at the funeral home. Everything was a blur and she did not have the patience to make any decisions. She held on with a really tight grip to his kacky shorts, fishing hat and the white colored shirt she never had the opportunity to give him for Christmas. When the director spoke, she saw his lips move, but could not hear a thing. Numbness infected her heart, holding each piece together through the funeral. When she walked into their cozy nest, emptiness echoed into her heart and soul as reminders of him began to poke at her.   Their home had his signature in every room.

A few weeks after Michael's funeral, Maria answered the door to a dark haired man in a blue uniform.

"Mrs. Maxen?" asked sergeant Adams

"Yes, I don't think I called you, Sir."

"Mam, we came to bring you this. We found it several feet from your husband's car."

Maria hadn't thought about his cell phone, nor the feeling of nauseousness that would soon follow. She raised her arm back to throw it at the large black trash can outside until a droplet of curiosity overtook her mind. To hear his voice and see his messages might fill the emptiness she was feeling ... She opened up the few text messages she saw and read the text she sent him when she went home after he had passed away.

"I was headed to the hospital to say I was sorry, bring him back home and nurse him back to health," she thought as a tear rolled down her cheek. "Instead, I felt an ocean of love roll out of my heart and evaporate into the atmosphere."

There were countless work emails and a few text messages. She began to go through them one by one. Maria wasn't sure she understood them very clearly. She had doubts from time to time but the longevity of their marriage painted a relationship built on mutual trust and unconditional love. It seemed perfect, but perhaps too perfect. As she continued to go through his phone she realized that those few times her gut whispered to her were right. She kept seeing emails that seemed coded and they did not make any sense. The FBI was trying to solve the case of a woman who was missing from Chicago. Maria continued to read more trying to understand why Michael would have this case in his email.

Could they have been married that long and she never knew he was an FBI agent. From what she knew he was a businessman. Apparently that was his cover. She felt like she was married to a stranger for all those years and it sent darts of doubt shooting through her already weakened mind. Now, all the business trips were beginning to make sense and the little questions and details came together. She realized that her gut did more then get full on good food. It had power and she could tell as she looked at his phone log.

There was nothing in his phone and his text messages were deleted often.

"Even though you lied to me, I'll Always Love You," Maria quietly said.

"I love you" came up on the screen. Maria wondered if it was him or if it was autocorrect.

"I know that came from you." Whispered Maria.

Maria began to think about when they were in their early twenties and they would joke around about becoming FBI agents when their children were grown up. She found it ironic at this point that Michael really was an FBI agent.

Maria called Angelia

"Hey, how are you doing sweetie?"

"Oh my gosh Angelia. Are you sitting down?"

"Yes, tell me what's going on."

"Well, I received a visit from the police that they found Michaels cell phone and the sheriff dropped it off."

" I just found out that there was a side to my husband who was a stranger."

"Oh my God he cheated on you, I am so sorry, that dog!"

"No, he did not cheat on me. He lied to me for years about who he was."

"So, what's the secret?"

"He was an undercover agent, Angelia."

"Like as in an FBI agent? No way, Maria."

"Oh Yes, Angelia."

"How is this making you feel? "

"Like crap, I wish I would not have known."

"You would think that the FBI would have taken his phone and not given it to me."

"Maybe they don't know what's happened then Angelia?"

Maria put his phone away to take out at a time she was ready and not bombarded with an explosion of feelings running a marathon to her broken heart. She then grabbed a blanket and went out to the back hammock to relax. The dead crow resurfaced in her mind. Maria walked inside and went to bed. She pleaded with God to take away her pain until morning came.

Living in a fog, the day seemed to go by quickly. Maria came home from work, took her shoes and her suit jacket off and began to cook dinner. Jaden went to the family room and sat at his desk to finish his common core math homework. Michaela went to her room to do her homework. Maria threw a noodle at the wall and the TV turned on at its loudest. Jaden ran into the kitchen with a blank stare and a puzzled look of uncertainty. Maria went to go turn the TV off. It took a full minute for it to shut off. It was a show about shark fishing. Maria began to get the chills.

"I love you Michael and I miss you more than you could ever imagine."

"Mommy who are you talking to?"

"Oh I'm just talking to your Daddy sweetie."

"Did he say anything back to you?"

"He said I love you Jaden and Michaela.

"I miss Daddy, Mommy."

"I know sweetie, we all miss Daddy."

"What's for dinner?"

"How does spaghetti sound Buddy, with garlic bread?"

"Sounds good Mommy, I'll set the table."

"You know what Buddy, that is very sweet!"

"Thank you, but let's just eat in the living room today."

"Your welcome Mommy, we never eat in the living room."

They finished dinner and yet another day of emptiness passed. Before they knew it, a few months would pass by.

One day, Maria walked into school and Mr. Walker approached her.

"I heard you are not going to be with us next year?"

"Nope I am going to teach in Chicago, Mr. Walker."

"Awesome, you need to get out, experiment and explore life. Life is so short, Maria."

"I know, but it is scary to."

"All changes are scary. Call me if you need to talk, Maria."

"How are you doing? I heard you got in trouble recently for doing a project that was on the line of a policy?"

"Boy, news travels fast and yeah, dumb decision on my part, I am still beating myself up for it."

"Why are you still beating yourself up?"

"Because, I hate to fail."

"You know, failure is a part of life and it's supposed to be one of the biggest parts of life."

"I will keep that in mind."

Maria gave Mr. Walker a hug and left the school when her phone rang.

"Did I hear your message right?"

"Its time, Angelia, I am ready to start a new life. I have to sell this house and start living. I'm excited about this new job and can't wait to start. I told the school I was not returning in the fall. This is a great opportunity for me to inspire some kids."

"What about your kid's Maria? Won't they miss all their friends and family? What do yours and Michael's parents think about it?"

"It doesn't matter what they think, this is my family and our life. They will be fine Angelia, kids adjust quickly."

"Ok, well we will miss you."

"We will miss you too but we will only be 5 hours away, Angelia.

2

The morning returned and Maria thought she would take some time out for herself. She drove to a deserted trail a few miles past her house.   About a mile on her run, she approached an abandoned windy dirt path, calling her wild heart to explore. She felt like she had spent hours climbing over lifeless limbs resting throughout the heart of the woods. The large, freshly fallen one presented her with an obstacle which tempted her to turn around. After a tiny scuffle as she climbed over it, Maria's heart filled with joy. She felt free to rest a spell in the open field ahead and took a keen interest in how majestically the pond reflected the shades of green and brown across the surface of the water. Sitting on top of the large fallen limb was a wrinkled man with rose stained cheeks, wearing a straw hat. The pant legs of his bibs were rolled up to his knees.   Maria watched him, hoping to not catch his attention before crinkling the leaves in front of her. As soon as his eyes connected with hers, fear carried away her curiosity.

"Hi there young lady!"

"Hi…Are you fishing sir?'

"Yes mam, I got a catfish, would you like to join me?"

"You know, I have so much to do."

"You look like you need to loosen up and live a little, mam. What's your name?"

"Excuse me, I live just fine. Maria's the name."

"Ok, well get in the boat and live some more."

Maria could tell he meant well.

"So tell me about yourself, Sir."

"My name is Gil, and I live about 5 miles from here with my wife. Have you ever been fishing before?"

"Yes, a few times."

"Where is your wife?"

"She is at home with my daughter, resting."

"How come she is not fishing with you?"

"My wife has a hard time getting out of bed."

"I'm sorry to hear this, Gil."

About an hour of Gil sharing memories about him and his wife had Maria reminiscing about the time Michael taught her how to gut a fish.

They had been out all day. Maria laid back on the boat and let the sun blanket her while Michael fished. Michael's face and shoulders resembled a lobster. Maria still had dried mud in her hair and all over her from Michaels mischievous, yet playful attempt to sneak a kiss in.

They returned to the campsite and he began the process of gutting and cutting the blue gill and croppy. She took no pleasure nor even tried to fake it and he knew this. They shared a few laughs while he was trying to teach her.

"I feel like I've forgotten most of my dreams., Gil "

"How about you? Are you married, Maria?"

"I am recently widowed. It feels so strange to say that."

"I am so sorry to hear that, Maria."

"It's ok, I'm moving away and we are going to start a new life"

"Who is we?"

"Me and my children."

"Sounds like quite a change to make, after losing your husband."

"Yeah, but we will all adjust. Plus it's a good opportunity to get our minds off of him and onto helping some kids.

"Are you sure you should take your mind off of him?"

"I'm a strong woman and I can do anything I set my mind to."

"Ok, so tell me some of your dreams."

"One of them is to learn how to dance."

"What would you like to learn?"

"I have always loved watching ball room dancing. I had Michael talked into taking classes with me before he passed away."

"You want to learn how to waltz, Maria?"

"I want to learn it all. I'm not the most coordinated individual in the world. I am very clumsy."

"Why do you think you're clumsy?" Laughed Gil.

"Are you laughing at me? I'm not really sure. I've always been clumsy. I'd imagine it's because my mind is often distracted with other things."

"If you spend your days thinking about the next thing, how can you really enjoy life?" asked Gil.

"I can't help it Gil, it's one of my hugest flaws and greatest gifts. It really works well for organizing and teaching. You sound alot like Michael."

"And you sound alot like Elena."

Come here, Maria"

"Why?"

"Why do you ask so many questions, Maria?"

"It's just the nature of all the women in my family. We are all very highly curious."

"Maria, it seems like you are a giver."

"Yes, I have tried to be most of my life. What makes you say this, Gil?"

"Because you mentioned moving to help kids. So why do you give so much?"

"Because I am obsessive compulsive with serving and would rather give too much than not enough."

"Well I find that very admirable. There are many people in the world that don't really care to give anything."

"Yes, my hugest weakness is when I give so much sometimes I can be taken advantage of."

"Do you want to know how to know if you're being taken advantage of? "

"It takes me awhile to figure that out. I'll give and give and then you know, 20 times later in fact. My best friend told me I needed to know when to draw the line. I am a kind person, but sure, I would like to know how to fix that. "

"When the giving does not make you happy, don't do it."

"Well, that sounds pretty simple. Where did you learn that, Gil?"

"The Bible."

"I don't mean to be rude, but I have got to run and start packing."

"Well, it was a pleasure to meet you, young lady. Maybe we will meet again someday?"

"I will be back to visit often. I am sure we will cross paths again."

Gil startled Maria and gave her the hug she needed to brighten her spirit. She left the boat and started her walk back to her car.

Maria's mom called.

"Hey mommacita, what's shakin?"

"Oh, nothing, just thinking about you hun. Babe, are you sure you want to move to Chicago? It is a lot different than it is here."

"Mom, I just don't want to hear anymore lecturing. I can't stay here anymore."

"Have you thought about going to counseling?"

"I don't need a shrink, I need a break from all the memories."

"How about the house?"

"I have it up for sale for now. It's so much to take care of. I just can't do the yard, trimming the hedges, keeping up with the pool. Then there is cleaning all the rooms in such a huge house."

"Ok babe, we support you in your decision."

"Thank you, mom."

"Is it ok for the kids to stay with you a few weeks while I get some stuff arranged up North?"

"You know we are there for you, Maria"

"Thank you, Mom,"

Maria went home and packed before picking up the kids from Angelia and Brody's house.

"Mom, I don't want to move."

"Don't cry, Buddy, it'll be good for us."

"Maybe for you, Mom, but not for us. I am a freshman and have gone to this school all my life. Now I have to move somewhere I don't know anyone!"

"Welcome to the real world. You will adjust!"

"I am not going to make any friends, Mom!"

"Yes, you will."

"I don't think you get it Mom, if we move, I will not be happy."

"Well, so be it Michaela. We are going whether you like it or not."

Michaela ran upstairs, slammed the door and started to cry. Jaden ran to her room, opened the door and embraced her.

"I don't want to move away from our family or this house."

"I know Buddy, but Mommy is not going to change her mind. Do you want to watch a movie in my room tonight?"

"Sure, can we watch "Puppy Adventures?"

"Of course, Buddy."

Maria came up the stairs, knocked on the door and walked in.

"Guys, I don't like arguing and I know it isn't easy to leave your Mamaw, Papaw and Clarissa, but will you please give it a chance?"

"Do you think you will stop crying at night, Mommy?"

"Yes, Jaden I think I will cry much less."

"Ok, I will give it a year, but after that, if I don't like it, I want to move back in with Mamaw."

"It's a deal, Michaela. Would you like to help me pack?"

"How about when "Puppy Adventures" is over? I promised Jaden I would watch it with him."

"Ok."

3

Maria arrived into Chicago to do some exploring alone. Michael always did the driving whenever they went into the city, so this was her chance to take on a new challenge. He would tell her he wanted to give her a break but she would catch him hanging on tight to the side handles. His eyes would pop out of his head and his teeth clenched down on his tongue whenever she drove them around in the bigger cities. Maria GPS'ed the address of the school and after a few angry drivers waved the birdie and honked their horns she finally pulled into a small diner only a few blocks away from the school.

"How many?"

"Just me, this time."

The waitress sat her in a booth and she took the side that faced the door this time.

"Where are you headed, why is it just you and what do you want to drink Mam?"

Showing the waitress her note with the address, she said "I am looking for the new school I will be teaching at and I am craving a beef roll with green peppers, onions, mozzarella cheese and water. Would you by chance have one of those?"

"The high school or junior high and yes, we happen to have the best beef roll in Chicago."

"The high school."

"You are only a few blocks away."

"Awesome."

"Now girl, you be careful."

"Always am, but why are you saying this?"

"You know, where you are teaching there have been a few shootings happen?"

"Huh…shootings?"

"Where are you from? Surely you knew this before you accepted your job?"

Maria felt like she was flying down a rollercoaster at 100 miles per hour and doubts began to buzz and swarm around her mind. She jumped up from her booth, paid her bill and flew out the door to escape the fight. Maria looked across the street and heard what sounded like fireworks. Shaking, she drove a block down, noticing bars on some of the windows. In front of the building was a man chasing another man pointing his gun at him.

"Oh, my!" Maria thought.

Maria finally made it to the school and met Ms. Waters in the parking lot.

"Ms. Waters?"

"Yes, this is me. Ms. Maria?"

Upon seeing several windows with broken glass, she wondered what the story was behind it. Graffiti covered the brick wall of the door she walked through. That feeling in the middle of her stomach was becoming all too familiar for her as she walked onto the dingy, dirt stained floor. There was no white board, it was an old chalk board and the desks were outdated as well. Maria's excitement for her new adventure was slowly fading into a "what the heck am I doing?" mindset.

"So, what do you think?" asked Ms. Waters.

"Um... looks good, well I am a little concerned. Can you tell me what happened with the windows?"

"Back a few months ago there was a drive by shooting. The windows were hit and shattered."

"You say it so calmly, these things don't happen in the small town I live in. Does the school plan on fixing them?"

"It doesn't happen regularly, but there is a lot of crime around here. We have someone coming next week to fix them. "

"I will look for a home and be ready by the start of the semester."

"Excellent, Ms. Maxen."

Maria left with disappointment filling her eyes from the back of her soul. She knew that this was not going to be a transition she ever anticipated and an ocean of discomfort flooded her mind. She decided to check out a few rental houses in the South Suburbs. She walked into the 1st apartment and sprinted out twice as fast as she walked in. A hot rush of panic began to spread throughout her trembling body.

"Ah, why did I not think of this sooner? I can go online." She thought.

After some searching, she found the perfect place. She drove to a quaint little town about an hour from the city with a corner grocery store and a gas station. She pulled into the driveway of a 3 bedroom brick house in a calm and inviting neighborhood.

"Hi there? Maria? I am Sara. The owners are looking to rent this home. Would you like to take a tour?"

"Sure."

She walked into a cozy living room with a fire place that projected a vision to her of the kid's shadows reading in front of the fire. Her imagination ran a marathon with how they would make this their home.

"So, what do you think, Maria?"

"Let me tell you, this beats all the properties I saw today. I will take it."

"Fantastic! I know the owners will be thrilled!"

"Awesome, do you have a lease to sign?

"I do, and I will email it to you, if that is ok?"

"Yes, that is fine."

As Maria drove home, her excitement began to fade. How she was feeling about her new life could be compared to the turbulence in the take off of a flight. After she finally arrived home, she spent her evening safely tucked away in her cocoon under a warm, blanket with a migraine like she had never experienced. Deep reflections from the waitress at the diner, the man shooting, the windows and the principal filled her mind with countless doubts. Reflections and thoughts about what kind of encouragement Michael would offer overflowed her already full mind. Nothing ever seemed to faze him. Although, he had been hiding his career for quite some time, she wondered what other things he might have been hiding. Thoughts took turns jabbing at her faith in his love for her.

"Hi guys!"

"Hi Mommy!" yelled Jaden

"How was your trip?" Asked Michaela.

"It was great, Jaden."

"That did not sound convincing, Are you sure you still want to move that far away sweetie?" Asked Maria's mom.

"Yes, mom, I love teaching and think this is what God wants me to do. Plus, I just need to get away and clear my thoughts Mom."

"What thoughts do you need to clear? Have you thought of seeing grief counselor."

"I told you once, I do not need to see a counselor."

"Ok, Maria, your dad and I support you in your decisions but of course, we will miss you guys."

"We'll miss you too, Mom.   We'll visit often."

Maria and the kids went home and as they walked toward the steps, Michaela screamed.

"What's the matter Michaela?"

"There's a fricking snake!"

"Omg, Omg, Omg, I hate snakes! Let's go to the front door. Where the hell are you Michael?" Maria gasped.

"You guys stay in the house! I am going to get a shovel!"

She wasn't sure whether it was a rattle snake or a copperhead, but she knew it was much larger then any she ever wanted to deal with. As it slithered onto the porch, she pondered leaving it alone, but her protective instinct took over.

"Michaela, look up animal control's phone number."

"A little bossy, there Mom."

"Michaela, no time for being perfect."

"Ok, ok mom, 999-9999"

Maria dialed the number and no one answered.

"Ugh, why do I always have problems with people picking up their damn phone?"

"Because you frantically panic, Mom."

"Daddy would have got that snake out of our yard, Mommy,"

"Thank you for this reminder…I suck at handling snakes."

"Woah, mom, what an attitude."

"Michaela, this is not attitude, this is intense fear. Snakes are my hugest fear!"

"We know mom, trust us, we know all your fears."

Maria tried animal control and there was still no answer.

"Alright guys, go inside the house. I'm going to take care of this situation"

Maria grabbed a shovel on her way out the door.

"Do you think Mommy will kill it Michaela?"

"No, she's too afraid and cautious."

"Did you see that Michaela?"

"Yep, maybe I was wrong about the cautious part. I have never seen mom pull the shovel back and kill a snake like that before and she did it in a dress. She's a hero Jaden. You know the only animal mom has ever killed was a rabbit and a deer. "

"She killed a rabbit and deer?"

"Jaden, you know she would never intentionally kill an animal, but she did on accident a couple times."

Maria walked in a bit frazzled scratching her head.

"You got him Mommy!"

"Yes Jaden, don't you try this ever, babe...Are you guys ready to pack?"

"Not really, Mom."

"Are you going to get on it?

"I would much rather you take me to go get my eyebrows waxed."

"Michaela, how many times have we talked about packing?"

"A lot, Mom, A lot!"

"Phone!"

"But Mom, you know you'll forget about it and give it back to me tomorrow."

"Michaela, we don't have time for this and not this time. No phone til you get your packing done."

"Fine."

A few hours passed and Michaela walked into Maria's room.

"Are you done, Michaela?"

"Nope, Mom."

"I hope you're joking, your phone has been buzzing, beeping and twirping all night."

"Can I have my phone back?"

"Here, catch."

"I have been texting you for an hour."Texted Clarissa.

"I can't believe you have to move! My mom and dad were talking about it last night."

"What do they think, Clarissa?"

"They think she is making a big mistake, but don't tell her." Said Clarissa.

"I know, Mommy really wants to go and we want her to be happy."

"You think you will come back?"

"I hope one day. We will come back and visit. I heard Mommy say to Mamaw that we would come back and visit.

"I love you and will miss you."

"I love you and will miss you too. You wanna come over tomorrow and say goodbye?"

"Sure."

The sunlight peeked into the patio doors where Clarissa met Michaela and Jaden.

"Look what Mommy killed Clarissa!"

"Wow, Jaden, your mom hates snakes!"

"Right!"

"Let's go to the bridge, Clarissa and Jaden!"

When they reached the wooden bridge, Clarissa laid her head on Michaela's shoulder.

"High school will not be the same without you. We were supposed to do high school together."

"I know. First we lost Daddy and now we have to lose Mamaw, Papaw and our best friends, Clarissa. Promise me we will do college together?"

Clarissa whispered with tears in her eyes, "I promise."

"Time to start loading the truck, kids!"

"Who is driving the truck, Maria?" Asked Clarissa.

"I am Clarissa?"

"Woah, has your mom ever drove one of those beasts?"

"Nope...Wish us luck, Clarissa!"

"Your mom is driving in the city and a large moving van? You guys are brave!"

"Very funny, Clarissa!" Let's roll, kids!"

They said goodbye and headed up North.

"Are you guy's hungry?"

"Yes, Mommy, very!"

"How about you, Michaela?"

Michaela could not hear her with her headphones on.

"Michaela!"

"Whaaat?!"

"Dooo yooou waaant tooo eat?"

"No, I'm nooooot hungry!"

"Ok, Jaden, how about a sausage burrito?"

"Ok, Mommy and an apple juice."

"Of course, Buddy!"

"How long will it take us to get there, mom?"

"5 hours, Michaela, you can check the GPS."

"Did you know it's supposed to storm today and tonight, mom?"

"No, I didn't. I'm driving to Chicago in a ginormous truck and it's going to storm bad."

It began to rain and the intensity of the storm paralleled the intensity of her anxiety as they drove further North. The pouring buckets of rain began to simmer down and they heard a loud noise which had them looking for the closest train tracks.

"OMG what is that, Mom?"

"That looks like a tornado! Look in the sky."

"Are we going to get caught in that, Mom?"

"I don't think so, but maybe we oughtta pull over somewhere til the storm is over, babe."

"Mom, I don't see any exits close by."

"How about we go pull under that overpass, Mom?"

"That's the worst place to go in a tornado, Michaela."

Maria could hear Michael whispering "Pray and have faith baby."

As the truck was shook by the increasing wind, Maria said "Pray Michaela."

"I'm praying mom, this is really scary!"

Both of her hands were glued to the wheel, of a very unfamiliar truck.

"God, please protect us from harm." Prayed Maria.

"I'm getting scared Mommy!" Yelled Jaden.

"We will be ok, Buddy. Whenever you get scared, just pray."

"Oooooh my goooooosh, did you see that? It completely missed us!" Yelled Maria.

"Woah!" Exclaimed Michaela.

They finally arrived to their new nest just in time to watch the evening sky paint its closing masterpiece from the porch swing.

"Although I miss going to the cemetery and looking at the stones, this is a nice place to watch the sunset, Mom."

" Do you think other families enjoy walking around cemeteries?"

"Who cares Mom, we do!"

"That's right!"

"How long do we have the truck for mom?"

"3 days."

"I say we get some rest tonight and hustle in the morning!"

"I can deal with that, Michaela!"

"When does school start, Mom?"

"It starts on Monday, Michaela. How are you feeling about it?"

"I am a little nervous, Mom, but I am not making friends here."

"Give it a chance, Michaela. I am sure you will make great friends."

"Come on Jaden, let's go get our plastic air beds and munchies out of the van."

"Ok, Mommy."

"So, what do you think of the house guys?"

"Honestly? It's much smaller than our house and the back yard is very small. Our rooms are a lot smaller too!"

"Yes, it is, Michaela but it will be a lot easier to keep clean and take care of."

"True, I miss Mamaw and Papaw already Mommy"

"I do to. We are strong and we will adjust."

"You always do that Mom!"

"Do what Michaela?"

"Try to make my feelings better. Sometimes I just want to tell you my feelings without you saying I'll feel better. Sometimes I just want you to hear what I am saying."

"I'm sorry you feel this way, Michaela. That is fair. I will work on that Michaela"

"Thank you, Mom."

Maria turned off the lights and Jaden started singing.

"Jaden, it is time for bed Buddy."

"Ok, Mom, I love you!"

On Sunday, the moon said goodnight and the morning sunrise came quicker than it ever did.

"Good morning Jaden!"

"Good morning, Mommy!"

"Seriously, can you guys be quiet, I am trying to sleep!"

"No, it's time to start a new day!"

"Since when did you become a morning person, Mother?"

"Just excited about starting our new life, Michaela and since when did you start calling me Mother?!"

"Can you keep your excitement contained for an hour?"

Michaela covered her head with the covers.

"I know we are really far, but do you think you can handle walking your brother to school and then walking yourself?"

"Funny Mom, I got this. I'm more worried about your commute. Did you decide you would take the train in?"

"Yes, I don't want to drive in traffic if I don't have to."

"Smart move Mom.."

Maria got off the train, walking about 10 blocks and finally arrived at the school. She walked inside her classroom to students pushing their way to their seats. Maria happened to hear one of the kids in the group yell "What the hell does this crap mean? This lady come from "sunshine city o' sumthin'?"

Maria walked past the curious group just as Jerri said, " I bet we could be her worst nightmare!"

"Maybe, I have had some huge nightmares, but then I'd have to at least thank you for making me a huge part of your thoughts!"exclaimed Maria.

Jeri rolled her eyes at Maria and walked to her seat.

The day seemed to drag on as long as her waiting for her soul mate to cross her path. When she arrived home, Michaela and Jaden were fixing dinner.

"How was your day guys?"

"Good,Mom." Said Jaden.

"You seem quiet Michaela, tell me about it."

"No, mom, I don't want to talk about it!"

"Ok, how about, you Jaden?"

"It was good mom, I petted a snake today!"

"Awesome, Jaden, especially since we are scared of snakes! I'm proud of you!"

"Thanks, Mommy!"

"How about we rent a movie guys?"

They went to the movie store and decided on "Humanoids."

I say we skip unpacking, grab some warm cozy blankets, keep warm, cuddle and watch this movie tonight!"

"Deal, Mommy!"

They all fell asleep and Jaden woke Maria up.

"I'm hungry Mommy, got toast?"

"Jaden, its 5am, can you wait a little longer?'

"Mommy, get up!"

Maria began to miss the days Michael would get up early in the morning with Jaden. They would often make breakfast, go out on the porch and eat as they watched the sun rise!

How about strawberry flavored jelly?"

"Ok, Buddy!"

"Can I have some soda?"

"You know better than to ask that question, Jaden."

"Ooooookk, Mommy!"

"Why don't you go get dressed and wake up your sister?"

"Ok, Mommy."

"I'm headed out Michaela!" Yelled Maria.

"Bye!"

Maria spent her first week getting acquainted with her students. Unfortunately, upon arriving the following Monday, she unexpectedly caught the tail end of Ms. Waters' bright red face 2 inches from Shanequa's. She was scolding her in a tone that made screeching fingernails on a chalkboard sound like distant church bells.

"What's going on, Ms. Waters?"

"Shanequa has been absent every other day this week, Ms. Maria."

Maria took Ms. Water's aside.

"I would appreciate it if you would talk to me before you ever again scold any of my students. I would guess you didn't know that Shanequa is pregnant?"

"No, Ms. Maria, I did not know that."

"Did you bother asking, Ms. Waters?"

"Well, maybe if you could keep your students under control Ms. Maria, I would not have to discipline them."

"Is that what you want Ms. Waters? Students under your control?"

"Yes, that would make my job smoother and much easier,"

"Are you developing future leaders? Or robots?"

Ms. Waters stormed out of Maria's classroom with a bright red look of vengeance and the pressure of bureaucratic rules waiting to boil over the surface of the brick wall that steadily built in her heart through the years.

Maria's phone rang.

"Hey, mom."

"Hey, sweetie. How are things going, Maria??"

"Things are great, how are you and Dad doing?"

"Good."

"Your lying, Mom."

"Well, we are good, I have just not been able to get my body moving fast enough. The shelter has been overflowing with people lately and my kitchen is a wreck of pots, pans and crockpots."

"Mom, how about you take some time to enjoy life and plant some flowers?"

"I am working on it, Maria, you know how important it is for me to give back."

"I know this Mom, but you give so much in your life anyway. I am concerned about your health."

Maria hung up with her mom thinking about the time she told her the story of why giving back was so important to her. Back when she was a little girl, her father lost his job due to depression. For a brief moment in her life, she and her parents found themselves living without a home. They first used the rest of their money to rent some rooms. When the money ran out, they moved into a small white church. They bathed in the kitchen sink and slept on cots. Family came to visit them with gifts of food. They would often visit friends and feel the luxury of a hot steamy shower. Every once in awhile they caught the reflection of police lights dancing across the church windows. Her mom would peek out of the squared glass window, with her pointer finger up to her lips, praying no one would see them living there. Then one day, their suffering finally ended when they found a home to move to. The day they finally had a home, a white dove flew into the church and landed in her open palm.   It sat there so peacefully and when they left and were finally free, it flew away.

Maria began to feel the most unsettling feelings about how many more times she would hear her mother's direct Italian voice speak her peace or how many times she would hear those sweet I love you's."

" Hey, Miss Maria when can I talk to you?"

"How about after class, Laquisha?"

"Sounds good Miss Maria."

"What's the matter Miss Laquisha?"

"Well, Dominic, he's been cheating on his papers."

"How do you know this Laquisha?"

"Because he asked me to write a paper for him Ms. Maria."

"What did you say to him?"

"I said no."

"Well, it sounds like you made the right choice."

"Yeah, but I know he's mad at me, Ms. Maria."

"He'll get over it! Im proud of you for doing the right thing."

"Thank you, Ms. Maria. I try to do the right thing but sometimes it's hard with all the stuff everybody's tried to do."

"That's what makes you strong and beautiful!"

"Do you think Dominic's asking anymore people to do his homework?"

"I don't know, Laquisha."

The next day passed and Dominic walked into class.

"Dominic, do you have a few minutes to chat?"

"I do Ms. Maria."

"So, Dominic, I heard you were needing some help with

writing your paper?"

"Yeah, Ms. Maria, I need some help with it."

"Well, why don't you write it yourself?"

"When I get home from school I don't have any time to write a paper. I take care of my brother and sister so my mom can go to work."

"Then, Dominic you don't have ANY time at all to write a paper?"

"I have some time, but I don't have a lot of time to write a paper."

"What about study hall?"

"I've been in the principal's office for study hall."

"Why in the principal's office?"

"Well, I got in trouble for smoking in the bathroom"

"When will those detentions in the principal's office be over?"

"After this week?"

"So, how about I extend your date of your paper and you write it yourself in study hall? If you need help with it you come talk to me?"

"You would help me Ms. Maria?"

"What are you snickering about David?"

"Oh, nothing Ms. Maria."

"I don't believe you David."

"Well, I just heard what you said to Dominic, that you would help him with his paper."

"Yes, I said I would help him with his paper."

"Ain't no teachers never help us with our papers. They don't care about us."

"Well, I don't think you are stupid, David."

"I don't believe you, Ms.. Maria."

"Do you believe or trust anybody, David?"

"Not really, Ms. Maria. You talking about trust, really? Where you walk out yo' fuckin' apartment and worry about being shot everyday? Ever been there teach? Ms. Maria I don't trust no one."

"Watch your mouth, David. No, I have not ever lived that way."

"Apparently you never had to worry about dying from a gunshot wound, Ms. Maria. You ain't know what real life or real fear is Ms. Maria ."

"Oh my gosh, you've been shot before? How aweful!"

"Yes Ms. Maria."

"What happened David?"

"Do you really want to know Ms. Maria?"

"Yes, David."

"I was 10 years old and my Daddy and I was walking to the grocery store to get momma some eggs. A man drivin' in a long silver car aimed to shoot my Daddy. He missed my Daddy and hit me in the stomach the first time. I fell down. I could see the look of horror in Daddy's eyes for a second. Then he shot my Daddy in the head and left me for fuckin' dead. I laid there and heard him yell "No one be taking food off my fuckin' plate."

"Glad you lived David."

"Yeah, it took me awhile to recover, but my Daddy, he never recovered. You want to know the saddest part about it all Ms. Maria?"

"Yea, I would David."

"The man that shot my Daddy was caught and convicted, but he later admitted that he made a mistake. He thought my Daddy was someone else and that he never knew my Daddy."

"So, so sorry, David."

"Sorries aren't necessary, Ms. Maria."

"You haven't answered me, David who do you trust?"

"Me, myself and I, Teach."

"There's got to be someone you trust, David."

"No one's ever really had my back Ms. Maria. Everyone make promises but no one ever follows through."

"Sorry to hear this David."

"No sorries Ms. Maria. It is what it is. What I do know is no teacher ever helped us with our homework."

"Well maybe this one wants to, David."

"I'll believe it when I see it, Teach."

"I believe in you, all of you David. Where is that chip on your shoulder coming from David?"

"I don't believe nothin till I see it, and I give it to you straight with no pretty packaging."

"You know you're right, David, there are a lot of people in the world who just tell us what we want to hear and aren't doing what they say they're going to do."

"First smart thing I've heard you say, Teach."

"No need to talk to me like that, David."

Maria went home and called Angelia.

"Heeeeey sweet baby cakes. Long time no speak"

"So, what's new Angelia?"

"Same Ole Shit, just a different day, Maria."

"What about you guys?"

"Good and very different!"

"How so?"

"The kids are tough. They don't believe a word I say."

"Remember when you found out about Michael, Maria?"

"Yes, well that's different."

"Will you ever fully trust someone again?"

"I hope so, but it will take some time."

"Well, I need to get off here and take Clarissa to piano practice."

The next day, Ms. Waters came into Maria's classroom.

"So I hear that you're giving the kids extra time to practice in class and produce their musical for the talent competition?"

"Yes I am, Ms. Waters, do you have a problem with that?"

"Well, as a matter of fact I do, Ms. Maria. That time they need to be studying vs. working on the talent. The talent competition is fun.

"I beg to differ, there is alot of learning to be had by writing and producing a musical, a lot of self discovery, Ms. Waters.

"Maria, it really sounds like a lot of fun, but what these kids need to learn is discipline and hard work. Perhaps they need to learn a little more about logic and structure as well."

"They need to grow, develop and be their own people, become leaders, Ms. Waters. They can only do that through self discovery, through creating. I'm telling you that MY students are going to get 20 minutes a day to focus on the project for the talent competition. What's up with your obsession with rules anyway?"

I just believe in following the rules in this life.

"Yes we have rules and we need rules, but most of life is imperfect. Nothing is going to fit perfectly. Sometimes you have to break the rule to follow your heart. My heart says give these kids time because they don't have time to concentrate on their school work. They're focused on the dangerous stuff that's happening outside their windows at night. They're having to work and take care of their brothers and sisters or don't have the tools to be successful. Give everybody the chance in class. If they want to win in life, they're going to have to do a lot of thinking for themselves and feel confident in their decisions."

"Ok, Maria, let everybody do 20 minutes every day to get ready for this competition but their school work better be finished every day."

"Thank you, Ms. Waters!"

" Ms. Waters, can I ask you a question?"

"Yes, what do you need Ms. Maria?"

"Well, I noticed that you've been really short with me lately."

" I'm short with everybody, Ms. Maria."

"Well, you seem a little more short with me lately what's going on?"

"You want the honest truth? I think that you have been trying to get the students to go against my authority."

"I would never do a thing like that."

"Why were you telling the students that it's okay to call and tell on the teacher if something happening isn't right?"

"I was trying to teach them how important it is to open up and be accountable and it had nothing to do with you Ms. Waters."

"Ms. Waters when someone seems upset, why do you often think it's about you?"

"I don't think that lowly of myself, I just know people really well and people like to gossip. There's been more than one occasion that you thought you had me all figured out, think I am heartless and you are so far from the real truth."

"What do you mean, Ms. Waters?"

"I have been through a lot, more hell then you can imagine.

"What are you trying to tell me?"

I have been stabbed before. Have you ever been stabbed Ms. Maria?""

"No, I haven't. Omg, that scar looks like a very deep wound. What happened?"

"My ex boyfriend thought I was still in love with him when he told me he was leaving me. When I said ok and didn't try to stop him, he got mad, grabbed me from behind and stabbed me in the chest. Then he left me there."

"That must have been really scary. How are you alive today?"

"My neighbor in the apartment next to me saw my door open and found me laying in my living room passed out. He called 911."

"What happened to him?"

"He went to prison. He pleaded for forgiveness in court. Unfortunately it doesn't take away the visions from the past or the routine check behind me. My stomach still gets queezy when I hear the leaves crackle outside my bedroom window."

" I understand that. I'm so sorry that you had to go through such a thing. Now, I understand why you get a little stressed."

"Maria I try not to be buddies with everybody because there are people out there that will burn you. I've been burned and so I'm very careful and cautious too. I can tell you are very trusting."

"Well, I used to trust people a lot.

"What do you mean by used to, Ms. Maria?"

My husband forgot to share a few things about himself before he passed away."

"Like what, Maria?"

"He was an FBI agent."

"What? You never picked up on it?"

"You know, there were times I got a little suspicious and felt like something wasn't right, but then I would ignore my gut. I really appreciate you sharing your story with me."

"Now, you know just a little tiny bite of my life. It is just a hint of who I am. Perhaps maybe now you won't be so defensive every time I question you, Ms. Maria."

"Ms. Waters I must go get some stuff done before I go home."

"You have a good rest of your evening Ms. Maria."

"You too Ms. Waters."

"Hey El Senorita Maria!

"Hey Mario, how are you today?"

"I'm great Ms. Maria!"

"Hey, Mario, I wanted you to know that the paper that you wrote was amazing. You have such a talent for writing!"

"Okay, okay don't tell anybody my secret and my talent of writing."

"Why so somber Mario? Are you ashamed?"

"Well, in my family we go to work and we work hard. The

men don't do no writing, because my family be laughing at me if they see what I write."

"Mario where did you learn how to write?"

"I've been writing since I was real young, Ms. Maria. When I was a boy I'd be sitting on my bed watching out the window listening to gunshots. Sometimes I would see a shot man being picked up by ambulance just down the block. That's how I coped with it all is by writing in my journal. They are packed with some scary shit!"

"Have you ever thought of writing a book?"

I ain't gonna write a book about all the shit I've seen. If somebody found out they'd kill my ass."

"What do you want to do when you get out of high school?"

"I'll be working construction with my Daddy."

"You aren't going to use your writing?"

"Are you kidding Ms. Maria? My entire family would laugh at me if I became a writer."

"What about College ?"

"No College Ms. Maria. I help my Daddy with his

construction business. It's good money."

"Yes, but it's not all about the money."

"Do you have a passion for construction?"

"In the real world Ms. Maria we gotta do what we need to do to survive."

"So think about it guys, what kind of musical could you create with all of your talents? Who do we think in the class would be great at writing the musical?"

"I told you Ms. Maria, I don't want to write."Exclaimed Mario.

"Maria, are we going to do this talent show in this class?" asked Shanequa.

"Yes I'm going to give you guys 20 minutes everyday to work on your talent competition."

"Oh man, what do you think Ms. Waters is going to say about that Ms. Maria?" Asked Laquisha.

"I done did just talked to Ms. Waters."

"She's not going to like that, Ms. Maria."

"This isn't about Ms. Waters and we have already talked about it. This is about creating something beautiful from your imagination and there is much learning that can be done in English class by writing a musical. I know you guys don't have time outside of this class so we're going to do it here."

All we need is someone to believe in us Ms. Maria. Thank you for believing in us.

"And you guys inspire me every single day."

"You guys can work on your homework and I am going to take a quick break."

Maria went to the teachers break room. She could see a teacher outside standing next to the big oak tree in the back.

"Hey, can I have one of those?"

"Are you the new teacher from down south everyone's talking about?"

"I sure am. What is your name?"

"Missy, yours?"

"Maria. Can I have a puff?"

"Maria, once you smoke a puff, you're going to want more."

"Nah, not me."

"Have you ever smoked before?"

"Yes, I smoked when I was a teenager and then I quit.

"Why do you want to start? Seriously, why start if you quit?"

"I'm just craving one puff, that's all, just one puff."

"I know for me, if I smoke one puff, I want another puff, so are you sure that you want to have just one puff?"

"Yeah, give me a puff."

"How is teaching going for you, Ms. Maria?

"Challenging, very challenging."

"Hey, can I have a whole one, Missy?"

"Here you go. Are you a smoker? I have never seen you smoke before."

"I havent smoked in 16 years."

"Watch out, you'll get hooked."

"Nah, I'll be fine, Missy."

"How did you quit, Ms. Maria?"

"I tried cold turkey, but my husband would get annoyed with my mood swings and would take me right back to the grocery store to buy me a pack."

"Don't laugh, but I quit with stickers on my calendar."

"Huh?"

"Every time I made it an hour without a cigarette I put a sticker on the calendar, til I finally forgot about the stickers and the cigarettes. Teachers like stickers."

"Whatever method works for you, Maria. As for me, Im pretty sure I'll need a long vacation and several nicotine patches."

Maria walked back to class with the taste of ashes settling in her taste buds, feeling like a busted open closet of cigarettes.

"Alright Mario you think of what the theme of the musical's going to be so that we know what the next steps are."

Alright Ms. Maria, we'll start this tomorrow."

"Yes, Mario, I am really proud of you guys."

Maria's first instinct was to call Michael and the minute her heart echoed in its emptiness, she distracted her mind to the things she needed to do.

The next day, Maria took the kids to school and drove into the city. On her way in, she felt the car begin to shake and knew it had to be the tire. She pulled over and thought about changing the tire along the interstate. It was busy, so she began calling a tow truck when a man stopped.

"Hello, Mam, can I help you?"

"Um, sure." Maria said as she got out of her car.

"Would you like me to change your tire for you?" Said the stranger.

"Sure, that would be wonderful."

The man changed the tire and before Maria could grab money out of her purse to pay him, he disappeared. Maria headed to school with just a minute before the bell rang.

"Alright Mario, how about you write the story for the musical?"

"Ok, ok. Fine."

"How bout some ideas, Dominic…Class?"

"I think about real life on the south side, Mario"

"Right Dominic. We got some hard core stuff we can write about. We've been through stuff most people have never been through and would never understand."

"I think that's an awesome idea, Mario"

"So… the storylines going to be about living and going through hard core stuff."

"Mario, that's a great idea!"Exclaimed Maria.

"So, who's in charge of the music?"

"Well, Ms. Maria, Dominic, of course. He a bad ass rapper like nobody else. He can write music, play music and he sing good too."

"What about a music video instead of a musical then, Shanequa?'

"Now just think what Ms. Waters be saying about the music video vs a musical, Shanequa!" Said Laquisha.

"We can post it online too. I am really glad you guys are getting excited about this. I'm so excited! Things have changed a lot since I was a kid." Said Maria.

"You always got so much energy Ms. Maria! What are you going to do in our video?"

"I am not sure, Dominic. What do you think?"

"You going to dance too Ms. Maria?"

"No, Shanequa. I'm not going to dance. I love to watch dancing, but I have no coordination."

"Come on Ms. Maria, yoooou caaaan doooo it."

"I tell you what, you guys get all A's on the next assignment that we do, I will get up and dance in your video."

"Oh, that's a great idea, Ms. Maria. Never underestimate us."

"Not one bit of me underestimates what you guys can do Dominic, not one bit!"

4

Shanequa, what the heck happened to your eye?

"I don't want to talk about it Ms. Maria. I don't know what I am going to do. I be having a baby and shit and I know my parents will be ashamed of me. My daddy's been a Southern Baptist preacher for years and my momma, a preachers wife. They be glad Im leavin Rob's ass, but not glad Im not married and pregnant. I feel so alone and I am so afraid."

"I know it seems so scary, like your world is over, but you are going to have that baby and she is going to fill your world with so much love. You will completely forget about Rob. In fact, you will forget everyone, sweetie."

"I hope you right Ms. Maria, 'cause I don't know how I'm going to do this all alone."

"Honey, it's better to be alone then have someone who keeps killing your spirit. You have your parents and you have me."

"By the way, Shanequa, I read your poem. It gave me chills. A+"

"Really Miss Maria?"

"Yes, Shanequa."

"Tell me what is going on Shanequa."

"He's going crazy, Ms. Maria, he be saying and doing shit to me that my Daddy aint never said to my momma."

"What did he say, Shanequa?"

"He say, if I don't do what he say, he got connections in his gang he used to belong to that'd slice me and my family open with a butcher knife."

Oh my gosh, that is not normal, Shanequa."

"What else has he done?"

"Well, he broke my angel collection with a baseball bat and then he say it was my fault for nagging his ass and that I aint no angel and I'm going to hell for being a hypocrite. I'm scared what he gonna do to me and my family. He be playin like he all powerful and shit."

"Most people talk the toughest when they feel the weakest. Don't let his words scare you. Here is my number Shanequa. You memorize it and call me if you need anything. "

"Easier said then done Ms. Maria. You ever had anyone threaten to kill you?"

"I know what it's like to be afraid Shanequa. A long time ago, I dated a man with anger issues. He punched me in the face and I had to get stitches on my cheek. My eye was black and blue. You be careful!"

"Really Ms. Maria? I would have never known this."

"Yes, Shanequa,"

"Heres my number. Memorize it and call me if you ever need anything."

"Ok... Thanks for being there for me, Ms. Maria."

"Your welcome, Shanequa."

Maria hugged Shanequa and left to go home.

Maria remembered the time she was victim to demon like dark brown eyes, smoke coming out of his large pointy ears and a blazing fire of rage . She was partying at moonlight on a beach with her high school flame and 20 other liquored up classmates. Out of nowhere, Jason lost control of the fireball exploding inside him. His anger finally erupted into a fist unexpectedly at Maria's face. It was all because of an innocent gesture of kindness she shared with Pablo, the foreign exchange student.

Her mother, with her Italian temper nipped that in the bud when she saw Jason at the hospital and pulled him by the ear with gritted teeth exclaimed. "Don't you ever come within 100 feet of my daughter or you will answer to me, young man. You should be ashamed of yourself! I'm calling the police!"

"I'm so sorry, mam I made a mistake, I am so sorry!"

"Sorry, that's all you have to say? Your mistake could have cost my daughter her eyesight. She will remember this for the rest of her life. I'm calling the police."

Jason left the hospital that night and Maria never looked Jason in the eye again.

Shanequa was having some contractions and drove herself back to the hospital.

"Momma, they say my blood pressure's up and I gotta stay in the hospital for 24 hours to get my blood pressure down."

"What was your blood pressure, Shanequa?"

"It was 160/105 at the Drs Office."

"Shanequa, baby, relax and stop worrying. You know that worrying make your blood pressure worse. I will be there in a little while."

"Ok, momma. I will see you in a little while."

Shanequas phone rang and it was Rob.

"Hey beautiful, how are you doing?

I am fine, how are you? What you want Rob?"

"Why you think I be wantin' something 'Nequa?"

"Cause that's the only time you call me. Where you livin'?"

"I aint gonna tell you that. You be callin' the cops and shit."

"Why would I call the cops on you Rob, whatcha doin'?"

"Because you a snitch. I aint doin' shit. This is why you and I can't be together. You sell me out in a heartbeat."

"Yeah, you defensive. You feelin' guilty for something. I know you called me 'cause you want something, Rob."

"I don't have any food to eat. Can you help a broke man out?"

"WTH Rob, I'm in the hospital with high blood pressure and you being asking me for help. You don't ask me about your baby or nothin'!"

"See Shanequa, this be why you no good. You always all about you."

Shanequa slammed the phone down.

The nurse walked in and said, "Are you ok? Do you need to talk to someone?"

"No, I'll be fine."

"Well, I heard you gettin' stressed and that is not good for your baby or your health, Shanequa." Said the nurse.

After drinking a ton of water and resting on her side, Shanequa's blood pressure went down and she was released.

Within just a few hours things drastically changed and Shanequa called her mom.

"Momma, something's wrong. We better be fixin' to go to the hospital. This baby's comin' now."

As Shanequa walked into the hospital with her mom, she could not help but still feel like a lonely fish swimming in a huge ocean.

"Hi there young lady! How are you today? "

"I think I am going to have this baby today." Muttered Shanequa.

"Well, my name is Martin. Get in this chair and I'll drive you to registration. Labor and delivery will come pick you up from there."

"Ok," said Shanequa in a muffled tone.

"Are you waiting on anyone else?"

"Hell no exclaimed Shanequa, that mother fuckin' asshole would rather sell dope on the streets then take care of his baby. We don't need his fuckin' ass!"

"You know what, Shanequa? I'm raising my daughter and son by myself. My ex left me and aint been back since my son was 3 years old. You are not alone."

"Really?"

"Yes, really...You gonna make it!"

"I hope so, because I am scared shitless."

Labor and Delivery came to pick up Shanequa and checked to see if she was dilated. To their surprise, she was dilated to 6.

"Well, Shanequa, it looks like your baby is coming today! We'll get your epidural here very shortly. Are you ready?"

"I guess so, ready as I will ever be!."

"Daddy'll be here in 20 minutes." Said Shanequa's mom.

"Ok, Momma, but I don't need him preachin' to me."

"Shanequa, why you so mad at your Daddy?"

"I am pissed at men right now. Don't start about this Momma."

Knock knock...

"Hi Ms. Maria!"

"Hey Trouble! Would you like some company?"

"Of course Ms. Maria, they are finishing my epidural."

"How are you feeling?"

Shanequa began to uncontrollably shake and then itch as her pain was dissolving with her epidural.

"Feeling better, Shanequa?"

"Oh yes."

"Glad to see you smiling and laughing. Why don't you get some rest?"

"Sounds good Ms. Maria."

"A few hours passed and the nurse came in and told her it was time to push!"

She pushed for over an hour and finally, with a huge sigh of relief, Mareesa was born. But then, she heard "Code Blue." and the Dr and nurses rushed her baby to the table.

"What's that mean?"

Maria and her mom grabbed Shanequa's hand as they anxiously awaited.

After a few minutes, they were able to revive her and sent her to the hospital NIQU unit.

"You will be able to walk to see her once you recover from your epidural. She just needs oxygen for a week or so." Said the Doctor.

Shanequa's dad said, "Baby, it'll all be alright, let's pray"

After the prayer was over, the TV turned on and off by itself.

Everyone in the room looked at one another..."Well, that was strange."

Are you ready to start walking Miss Thing?"Asked the nurse.

"I think she's still collecting herself after that little happening." Said Shanequa's momma.

"What happening?"

"Well, that TV is turnin' on right after we finished a prayer."

"Oh, you mean, Rose?"

"Who the hell is Rose?"

"Shanequa, watch that trashy mouth!"

"Momma, give me a break, I had a baby!"

"Rose likes to roam the halls of labor and delivery. She and her baby both died while she was giving birth in the 50s and had been hunting the halls for her baby all these years."

"How sad?

"She means no harm. She whispers love to the baby's born, shows up in pictures and sometimes turns the radio on for the mothers giving birth alone."

"Can I go see my baby, Momma?"

"Yes, I will have someone transport you in a bit."

Up came Martin to take Maria to see her newborn.

"Hey Shanequa, how you feeling?"

"I am doing better, ready to kiss my baby."

As Shanequa ventured into the NICU, tears streamed down her cheeks when her eyes met her baby's. She felt vulnerable, but she also felt such a selfless and indescribable love for her as she lay there breathing with her oxygen. She saw this little hero, already starting out her life with her Mommy. She held her in her arms and felt so much peace as she rocked her. She thought about how scared she was when she found out she was pregnant and how indescribable the feeling of love was. Shanequa came to visit and rock her many times a day and by the 5th day, Mareesa removed her oxygen, herself.

"Would you like to try to nurse her?"

"Sure."

Shanequa worked with the nurses till she finally learned how to breastfeed little Mareesa. She returned to her room to have a nurse walk in with paperwork.

"Hey Ms. Shanequa, how are you feeling?"

"I am good."

"Are you ready to fill out Mareesa's birth certificate?"

"Sure."

"What's the matter?"

"I don't know what to put for the father on the birth certificate."

"Do you know who the father is?"

"Of course I know who the father is and before you be judging me, I am a straight A student and thought I was having safe sex," Mareesa's Daddy doesn't want to be here. I am not going to put his name on the birth certificate."

"Are you sure?"

"Yes, I am sure."

"Ok, well fill this out and sign here. You are going to be ok."

"Thank you, Shanequa."

On his last day, although Shanequa felt a void of not having a partner there to share in Robert's birth, she made the most of it. She ate a huge piece of his cake, put on his little "momma's big boy" outfit and called her mom to pick them up.

After she was released by the nurses, Martin came in

"Hey beautiful Shanequa, how are you?"

"Just a little sore, but pretty good otherwise, Martin. How are you Martin?"

"I'm good, aside from a crazy getting ready morning with the kids."

"I just want to thank you for being so kind to me. I was really scared and you made my visit really good."

"You are welcome, Shanequa."

"Would it be ok if we remained friends and I messaged you one day when life is less busy? It may be 18 years from now."

"Sure, Shanequa, you can contact me anytime, I am a friend for life."

"You seem to be a good friend to have Martin."

Maria's mom pulled into the hospital and Martin pulled her up to the car.

"Take care of that baby, Mareesa and you too, Shanequa."

"You take care too, Martin!"

Shanequa brought her baby home.

5

The days began reflecting new shades of color for Maria and the kids. She had taken more walks outside of her mind and into the maze of her heart. Maria and the kids spent the night baking chocolate chip cookies with their favorite gooey white frosting in the middle and decided they would hand them out to the neighbors, John and Martha. Michael's memory began to consume her thoughts and she realized her anger for him had finally come to an end. She reached a sense of peace and realized that being alone was ok. God was with her and consistently wrapped his love and grace around her and the kids.

What do you want for breakfast, Michaela?"

"I don't know, Mom."

"Let's go out to breakfast, Mom. Then, can we take a ride?"

"Michaela, why do you always want to go out to eat? We have gone out plenty. We can't afford to go out all the time, especially not with the house down South not selling yet."

"Ok, Mom, no need to make a huge deal out of nothing, how about pecan pancakes?"

"and scrambled eggs with cheese and fried potatoes, Mommy." Said Jaden.

"Sounds good, Jaden. We will have to stop at the grocery store. Those potatoes in the pantry have sprouts growing out of 'em."

They headed to the local grocery store and as they reached the veggie isle, there stood an exceptionally handsome man with sandy brown hair and ocean blue eyes…Maria contemplated saying hi with more than just her friendly smile but the idea sent shooting rockets of fear blowing up inside her. She chose to rest comfortably in the coziness of her warm cocoon instead.

The man looked at her and smiled ginormously with his almond shaped eyes.

"Mommy, can we go to the park?"

"You know I am so tired."

"Please Mommy, Daddy used to take me all the time."

"I'm not your Daddy…Oh Buddy, I'm so sorry I snapped at you. How about after dinner?"

"Ok, Mommy."

"After dinner, they headed to the park."

As they walked around the little lake feeding the ducks, they bumped into the same man they saw at the grocery store.

"Hi…So nice to see you again."

"Hello, beautiful."

As they stood at the pavilion, watching the ducks swim, the man came behind, close enough for Maria to sense his mysterious ora.

"Hi, there, do we know each other?"

"I was just about to ask you the same."

"I am Maria. This is Michaela and Jaden, how about you?"

"My name is Damien."

"Nice to meet you, Damien, are you new to this area?"

"Yes, as a matter of fact I am."

"Where are you from?"

"Chicago."

"What brought you to this little town?"

"A new job and a house far away from the rest of the world, Maria."

"What do you do?"

"I guess you could call me a loan officer."

"Ahh, do you have any children?"

"No, I do not have any children. Are those your children?"

"Yes."

"They're beautiful."

"Thank you."

"Do you know anyone around here?"

"No, as a matter of fact, I do not."

"Well, if you need anything, I would be glad to help you in any way that I can. I just moved here too."

"How do I get a hold of you?"

Here, I will text you my phone number.

"Sounds good. Glad to meet you, but we have to get home and get ready for bed."

"Nice to meet you as well."

He had a quiet voice...His upper body physique had her eyes distracted from what he was saying for a moment.

The next day Maria received a text from Damien.

"Hey beautiful, how are you?"

"Wonderful, how about you, Damien?"

"Great!?"

"Did you need something?"

"No, Maria, I wanted to see how you were doing. Are you married?"

"As a matter of fact, I am a widow."

"I am so sorry to hear that, Maria."

"It's ok. I am doing better these days."

"What do you like to do for fun?"

"I love being outside, in nature, but I also love the big city."

"Do you like going downtown, Maria?"

"I love it. Have you been to the Pier?"

"No, would you like to go out some time?"

"Sure, but I want you to know up front that I am not looking for a relationship."

"I like a woman who knows how to keep the boundaries. She keeps me in check. What do you have going on this Saturday night?"

"You have no idea, but glad we are at an understanding and sounds good, I'll text you my address."

Saturday seemed so far away and Maria was looking forward to getting away with a male companion for a good time.

The doorbell rang and Jaden quickly ran to answer it.

"Hey big guy! How are you doing?"

"Good, Mommy is putting her make up on."

"Alright, champ, can I sit on the couch?"

"Sure."

Jaden went into the bathroom, put the old step stool up to the sink and scared Maria as she turned around.

"What Jaden?"

"Mommy, you don't have to yell."

"You're right Jaden, Mommy is sorry."

"That man from the park is here."

"Did you open the door Jaden? Mommy told you not to ever open the door to strangers."

"Yes, Mommy, because you were busy putting that black stuff all around your eyes."

"Thank you for getting the door but let me know the next time you answer it, ok?"

"Why, Mommy?"

"For your safety, Buddy."

Maria entered the living room

"Are you ready beautiful?"

"I am."

Damien took Maria to a dimly lit upscale piano bar in the heart of the city. One of Marias all time favorite things about this time of year was getting lost in gazing at the little flashing bulbs of light. As she switched her focus, she looked into his ocean eyes, fantasizing for a moment about running her fingers through his wavy, sandy brown hair. He ordered them each a Chardonnay and her words began to spill out of her mouth as smoothly as the wine was poured into their glass. She was in the middle of a love story, one she had never imagined. With his shy whispering voice, he said, "Order whatever you want."

Upon leaving the restaurant, from the moment they walked outside, to when her shawl fell off her back and kissing her goodnight, his gestures spoke "what a gentleman!"

She began dreaming about him and his blue eyes until guilt began to fill her empty heart. The last exhausting day she had with Michael, his loving words breathed life into her...but most of the time they shared a soul to soul connection...She was ambushed by a memory of the time they drove to South Dakota and made their earliest memories together. They found a few hidden small town restaurants to try and stayed in a secluded, A framed cabin tucked away high up in the mountains. The view of the snow floating across the mountains in the steamy hottub, while letting go of every worry had her feeling contentment. As snow flakes touched her nose, he played connect the dots. They finally came inside, dried off, cuddled on the couch in front of the fireplace and peacefully drifted off into tranquility.

A week passed by and Maria answered an unexpected text.

"Hey gorgeous, would you like to come over tonight and watch movies with me?"

"Sure, but I must warn you that I have a hard time sitting still."

"Well, I can help you with that, Maria."

"How, Damien?"

"Wine, I have wine."

"No drinking for me, I have kids and teaching in the morning."

"Well, come over anyway."

"How about a few hours? What's your address, so I can GPS it?"

Damien texted her his address with "see you soon sweetie."

"Can't wait, Damien."

"Michaela, Can you watch Jaden for a few hours?"

"Ok, mom, but it will cost you and do you have a date tonight?"

"Yes."

"With that same man?"

"Yep."

"Let me do your hair."

"You don't like my pony tail?"

"No, and please tell me you're not wearing those 3 year old aged worn out pajama pants?"

"What? You don't think I should wear these?"

"No! You don't dress like you used to"

"Ok, what should I wear?"

"How about that cute black dress?"

"No, it's a comfy watch movie night."

"Here ya go, mom. Here are jeans, a cute button up shirt and your black ankle boots."

Michaela wound tousled curls in her mom's hair and they found her a comfy outfit to wear. Maria made the kids recite all the emergency phone numbers before finally walking out the door. The gravel road to Damien's had her driving in circles of confusion with large oak trees guarding the path to his driveway. As she pulled in, the rather large castle like mansion resting on a hill had a mystical feel to it. There appeared to be a faint lamp light on in the attic and what looked like a shadow caught Maria's eyes. There were no signs of life for miles away. Maria walked up to the door with her eyes fixated on the attic room and she knocked on the brass doorknocker. Damien answered the door and when she walked in. The smell of Italian spices filled his very large, impeccably orderly house.

Maria noticed an enormous, gold trimmed mirror which reflected her Victorian style and the home of a well mannered and charming man.

They sat down for dinner at a large cherry wood table in the dining room and she wondered how he knew that baked mostaccoli with shredded mozzarella made her taste buds tingle with delight. Dessert was chocolate truffles with Asti.

As the night progressed, Maria took notice of his pacing back and forth to the bay window. It appeared like he was wandering around waiting for someone to show up. Her stomach began to flash turning signals.

She sat quietly studying his restless body language, uninterested in the movie that seemed to drag on. When it was finally over, she said goodbye and bolted out the weighted door and into the dark, moonlit evening. Maria felt him whisper up the nape of her neck.

"Can I have a hug?"

"Um, I'm in a hurry. Text me?"

"Ok, Maria."

Maria felt a little anxious and knowing the kids would be in bed, so she lit up a smoke. She let the cold air awaken her, turned up the music and reflected on what was going on with Damien. When she finally walked in, Michaela was sitting in the living room.

"What are you doing awake this late Michaela?"

"Just thinking."

"About what?"

"How much has changed since Daddy died."

"What has changed Michaela?"

"Everything...You aren't the same person you used to be."

"Yes I am, babe."

"You don't get as giddy as you used to."

Michaela walked across the room catching a whiff of smoke.

"Have you been smoking mom?"

"Nope, Damien was."

"Let me smell your breath."

"Nope."

"Remember how you used to write us letters and go to lunch with us sometimes?"

"Yes, babe. I will work on it."

"Goodnight Mom."

"'Night Michaela."

Maria did her rounds around the house, checking that all the doors and windows were locked and headed to bed to read. She layed in bed and caught a glance of her bible but turned the other way to her romance novel. The evening flew by so quickly and if was time to go to work again.

"What's up teach?"

"Hey Dominic, have you been thinking about the video?"

"Yeah, I don't think I want to do it anymore."

"How come?"

"Because, we aint ever done a rap video in this school."

David , and I don't want no trouble from Ms. Waters for doing something we not supposed to do."

"What kind of trouble do you think would happen?"

"Ms. Waters hasn't liked me since I started at this school, I sure don't need any trouble for doing something different she may not approve of."

"David, why do you think she doesn't like you?"

"Because one time me and Philip got into an altercation and Miss Forrest caught us. She brang us to Ms. Water's office and she never gave me a chance to tell my side of what happened. I was suspended and ever since then, Ms. Waters has never liked me."

"Dominic, so you are going to let another person sit in the way of your dreams because you don't think they like you? I know you're tougher then that!"

"Ms. Maria, I mean this with respect, but not everyone is sunshine and rainbows like you.　In fact, no one is like you."

"I will take that as a compliment."

"Take it how you like Ms.　Maria, I am speaking the straight up no filter truth."

"And I speak the truth too, Dominic, just with a smile."

"Ms. Maria, when you've been through stuff like we been through, we arent thinking about smiles and sunshine.　We are thinking about surviving. You know what it's like to just try to survive?"

"As a matter of fact I do.　After my husband passed away, I have been surviving every single day."

"Well, you wouldn't know it by that fake smile on your face."

"Fake smile, Dominic, who thinks my smile is fake?"

"The whole school."

"Wow, at least my facial expressions have you all talking."

"I'm sorry Ms. Maria, I did not mean to hurt your feelings."

"No problem, Dominic.　Let's take a day and think about it."

Maria went home, putting on her fuzzy pajama pants, disappointed about her days losses,　but excited to know she would see Damien.

Michaela spent what seemed like days endlessly searching for a dress that sparkled like the stars in the sky.

"Mommy, is Damien coming tonight?"

"Yes, sweetie."

"Do you think I should tell him how awesome, I think he is?"

"I would think that would be ok, Michaela."

"I think he's here."Announced Michaela.

"Hi there young lady. You look absolutely beautiful tonight. I love the bling. And you, Jaden look quite handsome."

"Thank you."

Michaela turned her head in bashfulness.

"Whatcha playing Jaden?"

"I'm playing cars."

"Can I play with you?"

"Sure, Damien."

"Dinner is almost ready everyone."

"What's for dinner beautiful?"

"Well, you're standing awefully close to me. Ribeyes, baked sweet potatoes with melted marshmallows and ceasar salad."

"What's for dessert?"

"Chocolate covered strawberries."

"You've really outdone yourself Maria. How was your day?"

It was actually pretty rough."

Before she could say anything else Damien interrupted.

"You guys want to watch a movie?"

"Sounds good, Damien."

They watched a couple of movies. The kids went to bed and Maria and Damien stayed up talking about music, antiques and their, families.

"I'm not looking for a relationship Damien. I am very independant and my husband passed away not too long ago. Not that I'm not open to it...I just..."

"Does that mean I can't hug you."

"You can hug me."

"Ok...its a deal...Ill call you tomorrow."

"I will talk to you tomorrow."

"Hey beautiful, good morning."

"Hey handsome."

"Would you like to come home with me this weekend?"

"Where is it you are from?"

"Down south. Have you ever been further south?"

"No, what kinds of stuff is there to do?"

"It's a pretty small town. It is a great place to rest."

"Okay, I would go anywhere with you."

"Well, thank you and you don't have to follow me anywhere."

"They journeyed the 5 hour drive to Southern Illinois.

"Look, there is a mall."

"Should we stop there, Damien?"

"Yes, let's look at that jewelry store."

They walked into the jewelry store and Damien seemed quite at home there, inspecting the diamond rings with a little magnifying glass he pulled out from his pocket. He asked the associate to pull out a necklace.

"Do you like it, Damien" Asked Maria.

"Yes, I love the necklace"

"We will take it, " Said Maria.

"I couldn't, Maria"

"But I want to, Damien."

"Ok, ok..If you insist."

They finished their drive and reached the country.

"What are we going to do first?"

"Let's head to my parent's house. How about we go fishing in their pond?"

"Fishing, I haven't ever been fishing." Said Damien.

"What is that, Damien?"

"It's a gun, Maria."

"Why?"

"In case anyone messes with us."

"It's a small town, Damien, who is going to mess with us?

"You never know."

"Ok, well keep that thing away from me, Damien."

"Are you scared, Maria?"

"No, not at all Damien."

"Someone called my phone, though asking for you last night, Damien."

"Who, Maria?"

"I am not sure Damien. I gave them your number. I am sure they will call you."

"You gave them my number? You have got to be kidding. It could be the mafia after me Maria."

"Thats not normal Damien. You are scaring me!"

"Juuuuuuust playin with you Maria, you are so naive. You would believe anything I tell you. That's how stupid you are."

"Stupid...Did you really just call me stupid? I will show you how stupid I am and then some. If you ever speak to me like that again...."

"What, Maria...What's the good little angel going to do to me?'

"Good little angel. What is that supposed to mean? Ill walk away from you, tomorrow Damien."

"You're always playing like you are a good girl. I know it's fake and ya think it's that easy? To walk away from me?"

"Yes, that easy, watch me, Damien."

"You really have no idea who I am do you?"

"Who are you, Damien?"

"I am your worst nightmare when you cross me on my path, Maria. I mean that."

"What are you going to do to me Damien?"

"Have you ever been involved with the Mafia Maria?"

"Never, Damien. I don't do crime."

"When you cross me, you cross the mob. When you cross the mob, they will hurt you, Maria."

"How will they hurt me, Damien?"

"When I was in my early 20s, I was with 5 of my friends who fell in with Jonny Gutierrez. You know who Johnny Gutierrez is?"

"No. I don't Damien."

"Well, we were finishing up with a drug deal in a parking garage and one of the guys was getting mouthy. My friend Hal pulled out his gun and shot the guy. He was aiming for his shoulder and accidentally got him in the heart. We high tailed it out of there as a security guard had witnessed the tail end of the scene. The police lights came racing through the garage. The guard wrote my license plate number down and called the police. They came to my house, arrested me and questioned me about it. I told them I was parked there but nothing happened when I was there. I went and talked to Johnny and he put a hit on the security guard right before he was supposed to testify against me."

"Ok, is this real? This all is scary. You are freaking me out Damien. I am driving us back home, am out of here and done with you."

They rode home in silence and Maria dropped Damien off.

Maria lit a cigarette and began to think about their safety. She felt like she was swimming in a can of sinking spaghetti and had no idea how to get out of the mess she had gotten into. That night, Maria thought she would relax outside on the back porch where she connected with her heavenly angel. As she relaxed and closed her eyes, she was startled by hearing "Sailing the Sea of love," play on the radio. She sprinted to the outlet to unplug it and it stayed on for a full minute before finally fading off. She ran to the bathroom.

Shampoo bubbles soaked her thinning dark black hair. Every muscle in her body began to lose tension. She stood there for as long as she could soaking in the warmth. For a moment, she thought she heard a footstep but the kids were at her friend Mallory's house. She drew her head back to the pleasure of the hot water drops trickling down the center of her back. Wouldn't a hot towel from the dryer add a little more sweetness to her much needed dessert after dinner?" She opened the curtain. startled by the presence of an unexpected face. He was holding onto his gun as his most loyal companion.

He said to her in a calm and quiet voice, "I am going to hurt someone tonight."

She looked into his eyes as his cold air blew in her direction. She saw inside a bottomless hole missing the inner callings and longings of his soul. His left eyebrow turned in the look of darkness. Maria's innocence was slowly drowning at the thought of her being shot and buried.

She yelled at him, "what the hell are you talking about? People don't just say things like that Damien!"

He haughtily laughed.

"Awe, Maria, where is your sense of humor?"

"Um, it left somewhere between my hot shower and seeing you standing in the middle of my bathroom petting your gun."

That evening, Maria had a recurring dream about a woman who she had never met before. She was wearing a nametag which read Regina Jones. She was unsure of what it meant but felt some sort of responsibility to helping her. A dark grey shade of sorrow covered her tired face.

Maria began searching through her social media accounts desparately looking for her name, wondering where she had seen that name before. Her stomach began to churn when she remembered it was the name of the woman who she found in Michael's phone who had been missing for a few years.

Jaden walked in and asked "Mommy, want to come read me a story?"

"I cant sweetie, Mommy's busy."

"But Mommy, please come sit with me."

"Ok, Jaden."

Maria wrapped Jaden with the love she had as she continued to reflect on her dreams.

"I miss Daddy, Mommy."

"I do too sweetie."

"Mommy, how come you don't play with us anymore?"

"Mommy is busy, Jaden."

Maria knew that there were way too many things going on in her mind to even try to explain to Jaden's innocent mind.

"Mommy, will you read me a story like Daddy used to?"

"Sure, sweetie."

Maria's phone rang.

"Hey Damien, hows it going?"

"It's great, would you like to go ice skating tonight gorgeous?"

"No, I don't think so, I need to talk to you. I am really sorry but I think we should stop seeing each other."

"Why?"

"I just think you and I are too different."

"Ok, goodbye."

"Well that was a little cold."

"I understand, I am going to get off now."

Maria hung up. About an hour later she received a text from him.

"Hey baby, how's it going?"

"Good...Why are you calling me baby?"

"I am really sorry...Can I do something to make it better?"

"Not sure, Damien."

"Ok...Would you like to get together and talk?"

"Sure, how about we get together tomorrow for breakfast?"

"Great, Maria."

"Why did you talk about hurting someone the other night?"

"I was just joking, Maria. I can't believe you believed that,"

"Is there anything else you would like to tell me?"

"Nope, just that I love you."

"Thank you."

"Can we get back together?"

"Let me think about it Damien."

"I am so sorry Maria. I should not have acted that way or said those things. Will you give me one more chance?"

"Ok, Damien just one more try."

Damien stayed all day and they talked quite a bit.

"I have done some really stupid things."

"We all have, Damien."

"No, really bad things, things you would never believe."

"Can you tell me what you have done that seems so bad?"

"No, I just can't put myself in that position."

"Have you beat someone up?"

"Alright…When I was a kid, I hung out with a gang and we all desparately needed money, so the leader of the gang, Rafael said if we find a bank somewhere in a small town to rob, we can come up with enough money to go to Mexico and live. I was a loyal follower, so of course I went along with Rafael's plan. We found a town with a population of about 2500 people. We put on our black ski masks, our gloves and wore camouflage. Rafael went in first and I followed behind him. I yelled for them to give us all their money and Rafael filled the bags…And then, we got caught as we were driving away. We were surprised how much money was in that bank for it being such a small town."

"How did you get caught?"

"They weren't as naïve as we thought. Some woman who worked at the bank apparently was writing down everything we were wearing and the license plate number to our car and pushed the panic button as soon as we left. We drove about 20 minutes before we were pulled over and arrested."

"How long ago did that happen?"

"About 30 years ago."

"Did you do time?"

"I did about 3 years."

"That does not seem like much time, Damien."

"They gave me a deal that if I helped them put away the leader of the gang, Rafael, they would give me less time."

"Do you still rob banks?"

"Nope."

"Are you sure?"

"Yes."

"That's good"

"I hope this does not scare you away. I need to be leaving."

"Nothing scares me, Damien."

"Nothing, Maria?"

Damien walked out of Maria's house and terrorizing thoughts began to swim in schools around her mind. She thought about him holding his gun so close to his heart and him opening up about the robbery. Good and evil began to fight for power, terrorizing her mind with broken thoughts, lingering fears and drowning doubts.

Maria ran upstairs into the attic to remind her what peace was and she noticed that her long, formal wedding dress had disappeared. Tears flooded her face as she wandered around searching for it. She went into the plastic tub and pulled out a picture of her wedding day and she saw a halo of light surround their faces.

"Mommy."

"Yes, babe."

"I don't want to go to school today."

"Why Buddy?"

"Because yesterday, Jorge said he did not want to hang out with me."

"How come Buddy?"

"I don't know, I guess cause I like to follow the rules and do the right thing and they don't. What's wrong with me?"

"That is a good quality to have, Jaden, nothing is wrong with you, Buddy."

"I am proud of you for wanting to do the right thing, and so is Daddy."

"You think Daddy is proud too?"

"Yes, I know he is proud of you."

"I miss him Mommy."

Maria saw his eyes wandering.

"I do too Buddy."

She gave him a tender hug.

"How about we watch some cartoons?"

"Sounds good, Mommy."

Maria layed cuddling with Jaden, wondering how many more times he missed his dad that she did not know about and how lonely he must feel with the kids making fun of him.

Maria ran out into the garage, with her phone, cigarettes in her robe pocket and her coffee. She inhaled and tasted the nicotine, enjoying every bit of it. As she walked back inside, she put the cigarettes back in her pocket, peeking around the corner to see if the kids woke up. She made her way to the bathroom and took a long hot shower.

"Wake up, wake up, wake up!"

"What the heck mom?! You are not a morning person!"

"Today I am, Michaela."

"Does that mean eggs and pecan pancakes rather then cereal?"

"Yes, Michaela."

"Well that might make me a morning person, unless you burn them."

"Awesome, Michaela!"

What are we doing tonight?"

"Damien is coming over and we are going to make dinner babe."

"There is something about him that spooks me, mom."

"What scares you?"

"I don't know, his eyes scare me."

"Don't judge him by his eyes."

"It's deeper then that Mom."

"Let's give him a chance."

"I will try for you. By the way, you smell like an ashtray mom.

"Thank you, baby girl. You can smell the smoke?

"Welcome Mom, and yes that shit will kill you"

"Watch your mouth, Michaela! Please Don't tell Jaden."

"It will cost you Mom."

"How much?"

"$50 bucks and Dad would be pissed. Actually, I'm sure he is pissed you are smoking."

"Deal and thanks for the guilt trip."

Michaela and Jaden began their walk to school. Maria took the train to work. As soon as she got on, people were aggressively pushing their way past her slow moving feet. She often read online books to make the time on the train pass. When she got off at her stop, she began her walk. There she noticed a man with a cotton cap and an old green army jacket rummaging through the trash. She gave him what was left of her sandwich and continued walking. Dominic walked into class first.

"So are we going to do the music video, Dominic?"

"Yeah teach, we gonna do it!"

"What changed your mind?"

"A little voice be saying it's time to take this high school by storm, Ms. Maria."

"Awesome, Dominic, just awesome!"

"Bueno!"

"Bueno!"

Maria heard what sounded like a loud rumble outside…And then within a few minutes everyone heard a gun shot. Oh my gosh, oh my gosh Ms. Maria, someone been shot! When people gonna learn not to be playing with guns?"

"Class, get away from the door and the windows!"

Maria ran to the door and locked it as her adrenaline shot up to invincible before calling 911.

"911, please state your name…"

She managed to get past giving the information to the operator before blurting out, "Someone has been shot outside my classroom."

"You all stay in the classroom!"

She ran outside to check the condition of the young boy gasping for a breath on the ground. He stopped breathing completely.

"Oh my God, I don't feel a pulse."

Maria sat holding the precious boy in her arms as he lay bleeding out the upper left side of his chest.

"Mam," did you see who did it and are they anywhere closeby?" Asked the 911 operator.

"I saw who did it, but not sure who it is."

"We have an ambulance and police on their way."

Maria sat there reflecting about how this boy was the same age as Michaela and there was a momma who was going to have to hear her baby was shot and killed. Her tears touched her hands and her heart rapidly beat as she anticipated the arrival of a terrified and grieving mother.

"The class walked out to their teacher crying and tightly embracing this boy, blood soaking them both as she repeated, "What's his name?"

"His name is Marquis, Ms. Maria."

"Do you know him Dominic?"

"He live in the projects Ms. Maria."

The police arrived looking for the shooter.

"Mam, can you give me a description of the shooter?"

"He was caucasian with brown eyes, wearing a black leather jacket. He had a gun and was aiming it at this sweet and innocent boy."

"Did you hear anything they said, mam?"

"The caucasian man kept repeating, "no one messes around with me and my life or I will take em down. You messed with me and you narked me out."

"The boy looked so scared of him."

"Are you ok mam?"

"No, not really," Sighed Maria.

Maria began to uncontrollably shake like the time she was given an epidural.

"We need you to write a statement about what happened."

"OK."

Ms. Waters walked into the classroom. "What the heck happened Maria?'

Maria fell into her arms and embraced her.

"Marquis got shot and died Ms. Waters."

"Oh my God, Oh my God."

Death began to wrap itself around Maria's mind as memories of holding Michaels cold lifeless body flooded her empty mind.

"I need to go home."

Maria bolted out of the classroom.

A shadow of loneliness was cast over Maria as she drove home swallowing back tears.

"Everything is going to be ok. I love you, Maria." Whispered her angel from heaven.

"I love you too, Michael."

Maria called Damien.

"Hello, Damien. Can you come over?"

"Sure. What's for dinner?" Asked Damien.

"I don't know." Muttered Maria.

Maria was distracted by visions of holding a lifeless child.

"What is wrong with you, Maria?"

"Noth…"

Damien interrupted her mid sentence

"Are you mad at me again?"

"No." Said Maria.

"Why do you look like you are upset? Lately, you look upset all the time."

"Will you just let me talk?" Blurted Maria exhaling the balloon of fire building.

"I held a dying boy Michaela's age in my arms today, Damien!"

"Well, those things happen in that part of town. You should be used to the shootings by now."

"Used to them? Used to holding a dying boy, another women's baby in my arms? I will never get used to that and the minute I ever get used to that, may God send angels from above to change my heart. Are you used to it?"

"I have been around shootings my whole life. Heck, I told you I was in the slammer for a few years."

"Cold and callous Damien, I can't believe you just said that."

"Oh, Maria, there is so much you don't know about me and one day, I will tell you about it."

"Tell me now."

"I would, but then I would have to kill you " said Damien with a frightening presence guarding his soul.

"I think this relationship is over." Yelled Maria.

"You know I am just kidding, Maria. What the hell is wrong with you? Do you need to see a psychiatrist?"

"No, I don't need to see a psychiatrist, I am not crazy!"

"Well I am, baby. You are going to need to learn how to trust me, Maria."

"Trust Damien? Trust is not built by scaring the crap out of me. Nevermind, this conversation is over. I think you need to leave, Damien."

"Come on Maria...I'm not leaving."

"Yes, my house, my space, go."

"Has anyone ever told you, you need to lighten up?"

"Has anyone ever told you to kiss my ass, Damien?"

Damien left and Maria bolted to the local park. There sat an old soul on a rusty, silver bench inside the wooden gazebo.

"Hi there."

Maria was taken aback by his amazing smile.

"Hi there."

"Whatcha fishing for?"

"Catfish."

"I love catfish. Can I take your picture?"

"It's been a long time since I have had a beautiful woman as yourself take my picture."

"That is really sweet. Why so long?"

"I lost my wife a few years back and I still talk to her every single day.

"I am so sorry."

"It's ok. You want to stay and fish with me for a little while?"

"I really have to get back home to my kids."

"How many kids do you have?"

"I have two."

"Kids just love me. Here is my number. You call me anytime you want to take the kids fishing."

"Thank you, they would really love that!"

Maria's stomach began to do acrobatics at the thought of going in to work the next day, but she knew the kids were counting on her.

"Mom, you seem a little out of it tonight."

"I am, Michaela, I held a dying boy in my arms last night and I just can't seem to stop thinking about him and his mom."

"Oh my gosh Mom. I am glad you are ok."

Michaela jumped into Marias arms grasping her firmly.

"I am glad you are ok."

"Yes, but the boy and his Momma wasn't."

Tears streamed down her face, swallowing back the pressure in her throat.

"And he was your age. I can't imagine how his mother will cope."

Maria walked to her room and layed down, Michaela and Jaden following her. She held them tighter then she ever had before.

"What's for breakfast, Mommy?"

Jaden stepped out onto the back porch.

"I thought you were making us breakfast, Buddy."

"Mommy, I can't cook yet."

"Ok, ok, scrambled eggs and toast?"

"Doooon't burn them Mommy."

"Me burn anything, never?!"

"Yes, Mommy, you burn a lot of stuff."

"Shhh, don't tell anyone, it's our little secret, Jaden."

"Ok, Mommy."

Maria drove into work and met Ms. Waters at the door.

"You will have a security guard here from now on Maria." This is Mr. Thomas and of course there will be counselors for the children."

"Ok, thank you, hello, Mr. Thomas."

Maria was still a little shaken.

"Hello, Ms. Maria, please let me know how we can help you."

"I will."

"So class, where are we with our talent competition? Dominic? Philip? Laquisha?"

"I say we make a video about violence."

"Who's going to write it, Dominic?"

"Phillip, Ms. Maria."

"Why you always think you the boss, telling people what to do, Dominic?"

"Cause I am a leeeeeader and yooou the writer and a damn good one Phillip."

"You need to be learnin how to follow, behind me Dominic."

"Yeah, yeah the only man I follow is my Daddy, Phillip."

"Who is going to play the music and sing?"

"I can sing Ms. Maria and everyone can be in it,"

"Ok, Laquisha, get to work guys, and let me know how I can help you."

"You mean you not going to work with us, Ms. Maria?"

"Nope, I trust you are going to produce an amazing video, and I am here if you need anything."

"No one ain't ever say they trust us Ms. Maria."

"Well I believe In you guys! You all rock!"

"Woah, there that sunshine again!"

"There you go, Dominic."

Class ended and Maria headed to the parking lot and noticed a man with a shopping cart and a can sitting on a bench outside the school.

"Do you have any spare change Mam?"

"I'm sorry sir, all I have is my debit card."

"That's ok, mam. Are you a teacher?"

"Yes, I teach English. What did you do before this, sir?"

"I was a poet."

"What happened? Why are you not a poet anymore?"

"I stopped believing mam, I could not find my inspiration anymore."

"I am so sorry to hear this sir."

"I would love to read your work."

"I won a Nobel prize for my poetry book."

"Are you serious sir?"

"Yes, Mam."

"Where did you fall down?"

"I got afraid and stopped swimming out into the ocean."

" Maybe you should do it again?"

"I have words floating in my head every day, Mam."

"You should write them down."

"I ain't got no paper Mam."

"Stay here sir."

Maria went back to her classroom and grabbed a pen and paper to hand to the man.

"Wow, thank you Mam."

"You are welcome sir. If you write a poem I will type it for you."

Maria left the homeless man and got in her car.

"How about chicken adobo?" Maria texted Michaela

"Yummm, Mom."

A call from Damien interrupted her texting and Maria answered.

"Hey cutie, how are you feeling today?"

"I am doing better, Damien."

"What's for dinner, Maria?"

"Chicken adobo. Damien."

"Great, I will be over in a few minutes."

Maria finished cooking chicken adobo and rice and they ate.

"Mommy can you read me a story?"

"Sure Buddy."

Maria said goodnight and tucked him in.

Just a few minutes passed and Maria heard Damien yell her name.

"Whatcha need Damien?"

"Your love and attention."

"Well, it will have to wait, Damien."

Maria walked out to Damien reading a book.

"What do you need Damien?"

"Nothing...well, your love"

"I think you have to show love also in order to receive love."

"I show you love Maria"

"You show me a lot of coldness, Damien. We are two very different people."

"I have to protect myself."

"Sure, but at some point you have to let someone in your heart."

"I need to spend some time cleaning my house. I would pay them."

"I'm off tomorrow, Damien. I don't mind coming over and cleaning."

Maria went over in the morning to find the house in a disarray. There were quite a few dishes and mounds of unopened mail on the counter. She looked around for security cameras and began snooping through some of his mail. The first bill she picked up was a brand new two month old cell phone bill. The second piece of mail was an EOB from his insurance company which showed quite a few charges from the hospital. Then she saw newspapers and pictures of a familiar looking woman. She was about to check out the attic room upstairs until Damien walked in to Maria snooping and snatched the papers out of her hands.

"Why were you snooping through my stuff?"

"Well, it was just laying on the counter, Damien."

"I dont care Maria. Please dont ever touch my stuff and snooping is such a trashy quality coming from a woman who thinks she is so classy."

"Excuuuuuuse me, Damien?"

Maria caught an extra set of mischievous eyes peeking from Damien's. She saw a vision of him ripping her head off and heard the hunger and groanings from his soul. She ran out of his house like she was sprinting at the end of a race and grabbed a hold of the cross hanging on her rear view mirror.

"Michael, I feel stuck in a very bad situation I don't know how to get out of and I am really scared."

Maria's heart messaged to heaven.

"Baby, stay focused and pray."

Maria put the wooden cross on and around her neck like she had when she gave birth to Michaela and she called Angelia.

"I don't know why, Angelia but he scares me."

"Does anybody know him?"

"He doesn't have any friends that I know of."

"Okay."

"Maria, when it walks like a duck it's usually a duck. You always see the best in people. Has he ever hit you Maria?

"No, but sometimes I get the most eery feeling like he wants to mutilate me."

"How long has this been going on, Maria?"

"A couple of months."

"You think it's time to end it?"

" Probably, but I am scared to end it, Angelia."

"What are you scared of Maria?"

"I am afraid he will hurt me."

"Even more reason to end it Maria."

"It just seems hard to let go of him, Angelia."

"Well, I have to head out, I will call you really soon and please be careful, Maria."

"Maria took a hot shower and as she got out, she caught a love note from her guardian angel in heaven. It read, "You are as beautiful as a sun that rises and sets, I love you with all of my heart." She could not even remember when it was written in the foggy mirror, but she knew it was a love letter sent from him at a time she felt immense fear. Her tears joined the rushing water as she thought about how much she felt like she was living in a different country with no true knowledge or understanding how to survive in its culture.

So much had changed and her life had spiraled so out of control. She wondered if she was the victim of a sick and twisted practical joke. She walked outside and was bodyslammed into the past with a memory of Michaela's 6th birthday party when all of her family was over. They played pool games til nightfall, grilled steaks and s'mores and laughed til she fell asleep.

"Hey guys! How was school today?"

"Good Mommy, did you forget to come eat with me?"

"Omg, sweetie, I am so sorry. How about Mommy comes tomorrow, Jaden?"

"Ok, Mommy, will you please read me a story?"

"Ok, I know it has been awhile, Jaden."

"Yes Mommy, how come you don't read to me so much?"

"I am really sorry Jaden, Mommy has had a huge hole in my heart and a lot going on, which is no excuse. I will work on it."

After they finished the story, Maria noticed Jadens tears in the reflection of the window he was looking through.

"What's the matter Buddy?"

"I miss Daddy."

"You know what Buddy? He is still here."

"Where?"

"Right there, Buddy."

Maria pointed to the upper left side of his chest.

"He'll whisper that he loves you and I bet he has already said it to you a billion times. If I was him I would tell you every minute I could."

"Mommy, are you ever going to leave us?"

"No, Buddy, I hope to live for a long time, but one thing's for sure Jaden, no matter what happens, I will always love you and I'll always be in your heart."

"Mommy, can I watch a movie with you tonight?"

"Sure."

"Mommy, why do you smell like Uncle jordan? He smokes."

"Oh, I don't smoke Buddy."

"Let me smell your breath, Mommy."

"No Jaden."

Jaden finally fell asleep and Maria skipped down the basement stairs her mouth watering for the taste of nicotine once again. Although it was not soothing her emptiness, it was filling her time.

As she walked out into the garage, she lit up a cigarette and began pondering her life. She was feeling let down. She lived most of her life striving to do the right thing and look what happened. She knew the hole in her heart Michael left would never be filled.

"Time to wake up guys. What do you want to do today?"

"Can we go to the park Mommy?"

"How about we stop and get some donuts first, Jaden?"

"That's a great idea Mommy."

It had been months since they sat at the bar and ate a donut at Huckleberry's Pastries. Mr. Gentry, the owner came by and did a few magic tricks for the kids.

"Donuts and milk on me!"

"How about we go to the park?"

"That sounds fun Mommy, let's go."

Maria took them to a small park in the center of town with countless rooms and ladders to climb. Maria sat on the bench.

"Mommy would you like to come with us into that building?"

They climbed up the little stairs and into a little room where Jaden pushed a button that took their picture.

"That was dumb, Jaden."

"Why, Michaela? He is just savoring the memories."

"Most of the best memories that are built have nothing to do with a picture."

"Great point, Michaela, but, what if you can't remember?"

"Then someone else does, Momma."

"You always have an answer. You are my child."

They climbed to the roof of one of the buildings and sat on the bench. Maria tried so hard to live in the moment with the kids but couldn't help but think about all the pain she had already been through. She knew the kids needed her heart with them.

"I love you guys so, so much!"

"We love you too Mommy."

"What should our next adventure be?"

Let's go down by that little pond and feed the ducks."

"That's an awesome idea, Michaela. I have bread in the car."

"Who just has bread in the car, Mom?"

"The last time we went shopping, Michaela."

"You always forget stuff, mom."

"Not always….Just often, Michaela. We are getting a head start, preparing for my future dementia."

"Niiiice, mom."

"Is school going any better for you guys?"

"I just miss Daddy."

"You know I miss Daddy too, Jaden."

"You know it's okay to talk about him, Buddy."

"It's hard sometimes, because when I talk about him I start to cry sometimes."

"I do sometimes too, Buddy."

"Are you guys ready to go home, guys? Damien is coming over tonight."

After dinner, Maria walked in the family room and noticed Damien reading an article about a woman who was missing. The day before that he was watching a show on how to pull off a smooth robbery. His short brown hair and well manicured beard had an uncanny resemblance to one of the most elite mob bosses in Chicago. She panicked for a moment and then wondered if her mind was imagininging this.

"Maybe he is just different. I have just never encountered a person like this before."

"Come watch a movie with me, Maria."

"What is this about, Damien?"

"Just watch it."

Maria was frequently daydreaming and worrying about the next thing in the middle of movies but this time her curiosity was leading. It was about a man, Anthony Cantonelli, who was on the run for a murder he committed and finally surrendered to the police after donating one million dollars to the homeless shelter.

"What did you think of the movie?"

"It was interesting, Damien."

"Me and Anthony go way back."

"What Damien?"

"You are the most stupid and naïve person I have ever met."

"Kiss my ass, Damien!"

"Classy, really classy, Maria…Just know if I go out with my Friday girlfriend, it is because you have pushed me there."

"I want you to leave and never step foot in my house or near me ever again. You are a piece of work!"

"Remember, Maria, I have connections to the mob."

Maria saw a vision of an extra mischievious grin float out of his lips and laugh at her.

"What is that supposed to mean, Damien?"

"I will leave it at that Maria."

"Ok, I hear you, Damien. Let me be perfectly clear, sir if you come near me or my family, I will call the police and for the record, I would rather take my chances then to live under your umbrella."

Maria's phone vibrated and she saw it was another restricted no answer. She was getting an anonymous call every single day for a few weeks. Anxiety began to seep into her mind. This was definitely not something that would just disappear if she prayed. These were the heaviest boulders she had ever encountered.

"Please take these burdens away, God."

"You must walk through the door to healing and I will wash them away, beautiful."

Ironically, the very next day, Maria saw an article on the effects of journaling her feelings. She felt like she had been unintentionally balancing a very fragile glass globe above her head. It was on the verge of shattering into a bazillion pieces. She began to write about what was guarding her heart each day and her confidence began to strengthen. Her mind was filling up with creative ideas.

Maria awaited curled up in a ball on Damien's follow through of the Cantonelli mafia coming to take her and her family out. Although she was hidden miles away in a small country town, she knew he could find her if he really wanted to. He had intuitive powers like she had, only he used them to mastermind bank robberies.

One night, Maria was having a hard time falling asleep. She

heard the sound of walking on her roof. She panicked, wondering if it was the Cantonelli Mafia or maybe a spiritual entity in the attic. She saw a vision of the woman again. She lay there paralyzed for a few minutes before messaging her friend Elyse who lived across the street. Elyse was a tough, strong senior woman who had been through a few spiritual encounters. Elyse came over and checked out the noises.

"Get away from this house!"

Elyse came out of the attic.
"I have a feeling it's tree branches Ms. Maria. It looks like we need to trim some of those limbs off your roof."

"Ok, sounds great, sorry I called, Elyse."

"Don't ever be sorry, Maria, both Gordon and I are always here for you."

"Thank you guys so much."

The next day passed and Maria was laying in her bed as she heard loud scratching on the walls in the family room. Her mind was barely holding on in it's newly created self preservation mode. To avoid bothering Elyse again, she called Jacqueline. She was at home in the wilderness of the supernatural and had a lifetime of taking control over her own spirit when surrounded by many spirits.

"What you need to do is bless your house, Maria."

She went in the other room.

"In the name of Jesus, get out of this house you do not belong here."

"You've got to take control of your house as well as your heart, soul and mind, Maria. You've got to make them mind and tell them who's boss. You are the boss of your home but also your life."

"Yes, Jacqueline, they just really scare me sometimes. Maria tightly clutched the cross resting peacefully around her on her neck.

6

"Hello..." Maria answered.

"I need to talk to you badly, Maria.

"What's going on Angelia?'

"A few weeks ago, I admitted to Brody I've fallen in love with a woman."

"Are you kidding me? How do you know this for sure and who? I mean, I have known you your whole life and I know you have had your fair share of fun with men."

"Remember that tall blonde woman from Germany who we met when we went to that little bar that kept trying to dance next to me?"

"The one who Brody was flirting with?"

"Yes. It started that night. The sun set and we all went swimming in the creek down by Warner's pond. She came up to me, wrapped her arms and legs around me and tried to kiss me."

"What? I was there. I did not see this happen."

"No, I didn't kiss her back but a part of me was curious and wanted to kiss her back."

"Oh boy. We have been best friends for over 20 years and you forgot to mention this?"

"There's more. I ran into her one night when Brody and I had a fight and..."

Maria interrupted her.

"I'm in shock, total shock...How is Brody doing, Angelia?"

"He was crying hysterically last night and told me he wants a divorce. He said he doesn't want to burden me or force me to love him. I'm sure he was hurt but he gave me a long lecture on our churches stance on homosexuality. I got online and ended up in a group chatting with a woman whose husband was having an affair with a man. He decided that he wanted to reconcile with her and they got back together. She said it's hard because every time he's with a man she questions whether he is still attracted to her. Then I messaged with a woman who was distraught about hurting her husband because he could not feel any attraction for her. She said she loved him like no one ever, male or female, but the feelings were missing."

"Sounds like you have been doing some research. What do you feel about it?"

"I'm not sure Maria, 20 years of marriage is alot to throw away, but I just don't feel any chemistry right now. I love Brody, but I am not sure Ill ever be in love with him."

"Didn't you feel chemistry before?"

"Yes, once upon a time I did. "

"Are you bi?"

"I'm a mess! That's what I am."

"You might be my crazy, friend, but you are not a mess. I can't imagine how Brody is feeling either, Angelia. He has to be devastated. You are the only woman he has ever known. Don't break his heart. Hes already lost his best friend this year."

"Michael was my friend too, Maria and what about how I feel? I have been battling these feelings for years."

"I don't envy you Angelia. I just hope this battle leads you to happiness."

"Me too, I don't want to lose my family."

"You will never lose your family, Angelia."

Angelia tried getting a hold of Brody several times, but his phone kept going to voicemail. Guilt and tears began to drown the make up she put on that morning

After about an hour, in walked Brody with groceries.

"How are you Brody?"

"Fine."

Brody walked straight down to his warm basement mancave.

"I'm really sorry I hurt you, Brody."

Angelia followed him down the darkness.

Brody did not answer.

"Talk to me Brody!"

"Whaaaat, Angelia!"

" I've realized how much I love you and I cant live without you, Brody!"

"I'm glad you get that now, but what about the many years of marriage you said you weren't sure if you could ever love me, Angelia?"

"I'm so sorry, Brody, I will never do it again."

"Really, how will I ever trust you Angelia?"

"I'm not sure."

How's about we go get a milkshake and talk about it.

"Don't do the cutesy stuff with me today, Angelia."

"Why would God give me this attraction yet never want me to pursue it." Angelia thought.

Angelia called Maria back.

"Angelia, I was thinking, maybe you should go to counseling?"

"We did that, Maria."

"What did they tell you?"

"She said the feelings that I have stem from the fact that my mom was never in my life and somehow I am reaching out because of that. That I am filling a void."

"What void are they saying you are trying to fill?"

"The void for unconditional love and acceptance."

"What is it you think you need to do then?"

"The therapist said that I need to be around women as much as I can and I need to do feminine things like cooking and cleaning. If I do these things, I'll feel more feminine and then when I feel more feminine I will not have the desire to be with another woman."

"That sounds like crap, Angelia! But you know, do whatever makes you happy. Angelia, what does Brody think?"

"Brody was crying in the middle of his office. He was released. Now he is often worried that when I am hanging with a woman, that something could be going on with me and her. He questions me anytime I go anywhere and the last time a woman waited on me he started getting irritated with her because he thought that she was flirting with me."

"Sounds like a hard situation for you to go through."

"With the children it is pretty hard."

"Sometimes I think I was born gay and sometimes I don't know. I knew a lady once who got kicked out of the church because she admitted she was gay and we live in such a small town."

"You have to do what you think is right, Angelia."

"I really feel bad for Brody. I love him so much and I know he wants me so badly to be attracted to him. I'm just not sure I can be attracted to him in the way that he needs me to be. I know he loves me with all his heart and it makes me feel so sad to know that I can't feel love for him the way he needs me to love him."

"The warm-and-fuzzy usually goes away after 6 months anyway, so it's not like you're going to have the big sparks and romance anyway, Angelia."

"Yeah, but imagine not having sex ever. It's a part of a marriage. Imagine not ever feeling that with someone, Maria."

I can't imagine how both of you are feeling and I am so sorry you are going through all of this. I love you so much and I wish that I could take away all your fears, pains and insecurities and give you the answer but I really can't. How are the kids doing?"

"They are feeling a little uncomfortable with all the changes. They can sense something isn't right."

"Well, you know I'm here for you babe. Anytime you need me give me a call, Angelia."

"Okay, Maria, thank you for being such an awesome friend."

Angelia and Brody walked to the local ice cream shop where 50s music was playing. They often sat at the counter and drank cherry flavored sodas. Maria looked down at the white and black checkered tiles as they grabbed a seat. Brody grabbed Angelia's hands across the red leather booth.

"You are the only woman I have loved for 20 years. Was there anything I could have done to prevent this from happening?"

"I dont blame you, Brody."

Up walked a long blonde haired lady with soft seductive cat eyes dressed in an apron to take their order.

"We would like an oreo flavored milkshake with whip cream and two straws."

Brody just looked down at his menu.

"You got it beautiful."

The chemistry between the two of them ignited an animalistic attraction which forced Brody to fly out of the restaurant.

"Wait, Brody, what's the matter?"

"You don't look at me the way you look at her. I can be smiling at you and I can't remember the last time you looked me in the eye."

I've known this for awhile, I was just in denial for a long time. There is no chemistry. I need some time to think."

"I understand. I can't imagine how you feel Angelia."

"I don't want to lose you, Brody."

"You think maybe you should have thought about it before you did it?"

"Sure, but somewhere along the way, I got off track and started believing it was the right thing."

"What do you mean the right thing, Angelia?"

"I believd that since it was with a woman it wasn't wrong,"

"Are you gay Angelia?"

"I am not sure, maybe I am bisexual.."

"Glad to find this all out now. I feel like you lied to me our whole marriage."

"I wouldn't say our whole marriage. I just wasn't sure who I was back then."

Angelia and Brody headed home. Brody jogged down to the basement and punched the wall. He then began thumbing through the old love letters and cards which were now meaningless.

"Mommy, is Daddy leaving? I don't want Daddy to leave."

"No sweetie, I am never leaving you. You are my angel."

Brody took off his cross necklace and gave it to Clarissa.

"This is to remind you that God is always with you, Clarissa."

"Thank you, Daddy."

"Time for bed, Clarissa."

Angelia tucked Clarissa in before heading to her room.

"I don't know when I will get over all this Angelia.

"I understand, but don't leave me yet, Brody."

"How many times did you cheat on me?"

"Twice, Brody."

"I know that's a lie. Why don't you just tell me the truth."

"You don't need to know all the details, Brody."

"Yes, frankly, I do, but whatever"

Brody put in a home video and his cheeks turned red.

"Can I hold you tonight?"

"Yes, I would like that, Brody."

"Brody's tears grieved for 20 years of marriage.

As Angelia came downstairs and caught a glimpse of his sadness, she broke down and cried. Brody was trying to fill the gaping hole she left him and she decided to take a ride to her runaway place and call her best friend.

"How have you been?"

"Afraid, but good, Angelia. You? I definitely don't have any room to be giving advice about love. What happened in the last 20 years Angelia? Life is nothing how we pictured it would be back when we were kids cruising town around in your loud Chevy Citation."

"Oh yes, how about the time we ran out of gas and that nice guy in the UHaul stopped and gave us a ride?"

"Back when we thought we were hot and invincible."

"Wait, wait, we still are...hot"

"You got that right sexy biatch!"

"Such a trashy mouth, Angelia."

"That's why you love me Maria."

"You know I hate you Angelia."

"I know this, my friend, I know this."

7

"So tell me more about where Maria took you guys the other day."

"She took us to the woods to inspire our writing. What you got against Maria, Ms. Waters?"

"Nothing. You know it is against the school rules."

"You so far up about the damn rules, Ms. Waters. I bet if Mrs. Woods did it you wouldn't care?"

"Watch your mouth, Shanequa! Mrs. Woods has nothing to do with any of this."

"I am finished with this conversation, Ms. Waters, finished."

Maria came into the classroom as Ms. Waters left.

"Miss Maria, I just want you to know that Ms. Waters was tryin to get us to say bad stuff about you, but I had your back. You've taught us alot."

"What did she say?"

"Why you be taking us to the woods?"

"Shanequa, honey, Ive learned so much from you too and thanks for telling me."

Maria took what seemed like centuries to make decisions. She knew she had done her job and felt this deep feeling in her gut that she had a limited time with her family It was time to high tale it out of the city. Marie, Michaela and Jaden began packing their things.

"Knock, knock."

Ms. Waters came to the door.

"Hi, Ms. Maria, what can I do for you?"

"Ive made the decision to head back south.

"In the middle of the school year, Maria?

"Yes, Ms. Waters."

"Why?"

"Ok, do you plan on saying goodbye to your students?"

"Of course. I will leave after the talent competition."

"Ok, Maria."

Maria called her mom.

"Hey sweetie, how are you? Asked Marias mom as she picked up the phone."

"Things are a little rough, Mom. I have been having stressful things going on with the principal and I decided it is time to come home. I feel like time is going by so fast and I miss you guys."

"What's been going on sweetie?"

"Well, she just doesn't like me, mom."

"Well, sweetie you know that people go through things sometimes and it has nothing to do with you. You also have to know that you take a lot of things personal."

" Yes, I get that."

"How old is she?"

" I am thinking her early 60's. Well I'm going to work harder on understanding where a person might be going through stuff mom."

"Okay, that sounds like a good start. How's everything else going sweetie. How are the kids?"

"Everything is going fine for me and them, how about you Mom?"

"I've been feeling kind of sick the last few days but I'm doing better."

"I'm going to be up there to visit you in a few weeks!!"

"Sounds good sweetie. I'm going to let you go and how about we talk later on this evening, Maria?"

"Sounds good, Mom let's do that I love you, bye."

Marie went to her class room to start her day

"Hey guys, I have an announcement to make. I want you to know that I have learned so much from each and every one of you, but I have made the decision to go back home."

"Whaaaat, Ms. Maria?"

"She be playing with us, Mario."

Shanequas face turned a rosy color.

"No guys, this is real. I will be leaving after the talent competition."

"At least you are staying for that after talking me into writing the video."

"How are you coming along on it Phillip?

"Pretty dang real, and guaranteed to reach people."

"What part are you playing in all this Mario?"

"El hombre en el carro, Maria."

"Excellente, Mario."

"How much longer before it is finished?"

"One week."

"Awesome guys! I am so excited!" exclaimed Maria, "Anything I can help you with?"

"I don't think so," said Shanequa, "why you give us all this freedom to do what we want?"

"Cause I know you will come up with something amazing." Said Maria.

8

Maria answered her phone.

"Maria, your mom is in the hospital again and she is feeling very weak."

What the heck is going on Dad?"

"I'm not sure, Maria. The doctor said the cancer came back, but with a vengence this time. She has a terrible infection. They can't do anything more for her. They can't do anything more for her."

Maria could hear the vulnerability in her dad's voice.

"I don't believe that dad, Mom always pulls through. How about I come there tonight. I gave my notice and we are moving home, Dad."

"Glad to hear, sweetie."

Maria picked the kids up from school.

"Nana is in the hospital. Can you take care of Jaden tonight and tomorrow, while I head down South?"

"Sure. What is going on with Nana?"

"Papaw said she is in the hospital and that is about all I know."

Maria kept her foot on the gas pedal, getting home in record time, cutting an hour off her drive.

Maria slowly and quietly walked into her mother's room.

"Mom, how are you feeling?".

She did not respond. She seemed to have already begun transitioning into the light.

"Would you like a drink of soda mom?"

She grabbed Maria's cup and reached to take a drink as if it was a can rather then a cup with a straw. Maria knew something was not right and helped her take a drink. She felt her mother's soul begin the peaceful journey, escaping out of her lips and flying to the majestic golden doorsteps of heaven. After being there when her grandma and grandpa passed a few years back, the souls beautiful departure to heaven was becoming all too familiar for her. She was becoming a qualified expert at saying goodbye.

Sensible doubts and denial held her heart back from speaking the inevitable truth until the pressure of reality finally blew out of her mouth what had become so blatantly obvious.

"This is not my mom! My mom is alert and full of life. Why does she keep falling asleep?"

The male nurse quietly gave her the look of "I know what I am doing."

"Are you ok Elena?"

Elena knodded her head at the nurse.

"Seriously, my mom is not this passive. There is something not right."

"She seems ok mam, probably just worn out from the cancer."

"Mom, do you know who I am?"

"Maria."

"Are you chasing fireflies mom?"

Elena continued to reach her hands into the air as if she was trying to catch something.

"Alright, it's time to take Elena to get some tests run."

"Ok."

"Don't be flirting too much with the nurses, Mom."

Elena laughed as she often did when Maria cracked a joke, said something unexpected and shocking or became Ms. Sassy Pants.

Maria left and called her dad.

"Something is not right with Mom, Dad.

"What's going on, babe?"

"She's just not all here, Dad. She is just not all here."

"I will be there to see your mom and the Dr in a few hours, are you still there?"

"No Dad, but I will go back. I just need to go eat. I am feeling a little light headed. Have you called Marcus?"

"Ok, sweetie. I will see you soon and yes, Marcus is on his way."

9

Maria needed some time to connect in nature with her mom's drifting soul. The idea of putting a burger in her mouth made her feel like hurling into an airplane barf bag. Instead, she drove a few miles to jog the long windy trail that led to the pond she first met her young spirited friend, Gil.

There he was all sprawled out with his brown fishing hat pointed down over his red burnt forehead and his fishing pole calmly resting off the side of his miniature fishing boat. Maria became very concerned for seconds but as she walked closer, his snores performed so beautifully with the fish splashing as they swam around searching for food. He was off in a different world.

"Hey, Gil!"

Gil jerked and woke up in a shaken startle.

"Gal!"

"Hi Gil, how have you been?"

"Good, well, ok. How about you?"

"Worried about mom. What's going on with you?"

"I am hanging in there myself, Gal. Rachel passed away a couple of months ago."

"Oh, my, I am so sorry to hear this, Gil."

"I miss her so much. I can't imagine too much more time without her, Gal."

"Oh, Gil, I am so sorry."

Maria hugged him.

"Do you think you will ever fall in love again, Maria? You talk so much about Michael. Will anyone ever measure up?"

"I spent so much of my life with Michael, but I don't think its a matter of measuring up. I think its a matter of creating something different and not comparing anyone else to Michael."

"After my last relationship, I prayed hard for God to bring a gentle, kind and inspiring man in my life. Thats all. I do hope one day he will cross my path. How about you, Gil?"

"You know, Rachel is a part of me. We were married over 60 years. I see myself making friends, maybe finding someone to Waltz with, but Rachel was my first and last love."

"I can't stay too long, I'm going to see my mom in the hospital, but hopefully I can come back and see you soon?"

"Anytime Gal, how is your mom doing?"

"She is not doing too good. I don't think she is going to make it through this next Christmas, Gil."

"I am so sorry, Gal, if you need anything, please let me know."

As she turned into the hospital, the red and white emergency sign flooded her with memories of Michael. Her eyes began to tear up as she experienced visions of the night her world had come crashing down into a million pieces. This was the night she found out he had passed away and cuddled up to his lifeless body.

"Really God?!"

Maria went back to room 222 where she walked in upon her dad talking to her unconscious mom.

"Rachel, sweetie, you are the mother of my children, the grandmother of our grandchildren, my wife, best friend, soulmate and the love of my life. We have built a life together that I am so grateful for. I have no regrets."

Maria walked into Elena's room, watching little sparkles of light begin to float out of her body. Showers of tears rolling down her cheeks and memories of the minutes she laid next to Michael swarmed into the entrance of her mind. For a brief moment, she looked up and screamed outloud.

She hugged her dad and then walked over to her mom.

Has she eaten anything?" Asked Maria.

"No, Babe, they have released her to hospice after she started reaching for things that weren't there and talking to her mother, Dorothy. They don't think she has much time left. A nice woman from hospice came, left a pamphlet and said it's normal for a dying person to stop eating and that it is her body's natural way to ease and soothe her pain. We are taking her home so she can watch the blue birds from the back porch."

The ambulance took Elena home and situated her next to the large bay window in the back of the house, so she could watch the birds fly over the lake.

"Mom, are you hurting?"

Maria cried as she made her way to the hospital bed in the family room.

There was no answer and Maria agonized over whether her mom could hear what was going on and what all her worries might be. She walked up to her, reading a prayer she looked up online.

"Mom, listen to this prayer, ok?

That if you confess with your mouth the Lord Jesus and believe in your heart that God has raised Him from the dead, you will be saved."

After Maria read the prayer, Elena's slow heartbeat had replied with a short song. Throughout the years, her mom made it clear that she had an insurmountable faith in God, but she would often talk about being really afraid of death. Elena's fears pierced Maria's heart.

Maria walked over to the old wooden piano, hoping to wake her up from her slumber and played, "Amazing Grace."

"Mom, can you hear me?"

At that moment, Marcus walked into the room.

"I can't believe this is happening Maria." Cried Marcus.

Maria hugged Marcus. He walked over to Elena's bed and his voice and the touch of his hand sent her heart playing another beat.

"Wow, Marcus, she knows you are here. In fact she gave you extra beats. I knew you were her favorite."

Marcus chuckled under the flowing tears.

"Mom, if I could do it over again, I would not change a thing, except maybe I would have spent a little more, well a lot more time with you. "

Maria walked over to the other side of her mom and her dad walked up to her. Studying her mom's long brittle pink painted nails, Maria cried as she touched the wrinkles on her mom's hand. She thought for a moment she felt a gentle a grasp from her fingers.

"Mom, we have so many memories and I want you to know, the whole package, the good, the bad, everything, I am so blessed and lucky for all the love, kindness, friendship you gave us. I know there were moments that we had that were painful, but I forgive you and I know you forgive me. You were my best friend and I want you to know I will be ok. I will take care of Jaden and Michaela and everyone will be ok, including Dad and Marcus."

At that moment, Maria felt a soft chill glide across her arm and saw a vision of her mother's soul awakening into heaven. She imagined her meeting her sister Pearline, her father, Gus and her mother, Dorothy. It left an immeasurable sinkhole encompassing Maria's huge heart.

Maria's eyes popped out of her head after witnessing one of the few times her father had ever grabbed a book off the table and threw it across the floor. He embraced Maria as they both felt a part of their heart disappear.

"Daddy, I have to go home, get to Michaela and Jaden, but I will be back in a few days. Then we can work on funeral arrangements. Will you be ok?"

"I will make it through," said Maria's Dad, his voice trembling.

Anticipating the talk with Michaela and Jaden, Maria's drive home was packed with countless thoughts and anxiety. She had just a couple more days before the talent competition to get through. Maria arrived home to Michaela's concerned voice whisper, "How is nana?"

"She passed away, babe. She passed away."

"Noooo, not again! Not nana too!"

"I'm so sorry babydoll"

"What happened Mom?"

"Her cancer came back and spread really quickly this time, Michaela, much quicker then we anticipated."

"How is Papaw doing?"

"Not doing so good. We will get through this though."

"I know Mom, it's just such a shock."

"It really hasn't hit me yet, Michaela."

"What's the matter , Ms. Maria?"

"Nothing, Phillip, Why do you think something is the matter?"

"Cause you aint your bubbly self, Ms. Maria."

"My mom just passed away, Phillip."

Maria choked back an ocean of tears.

"I am so sorry, Ms. Maria." Phillip said as he hugged her.

"Thank you, Phillip."

Maria wiped her tears away and quickly changed the subject.

Are you guys ready for the talent competition?"

"Yes, Ms. Maria. Laquisha got a little bossy, but we put her in her place and we done with our video.

"Awesome, Phillip! I can't wait to watch it tonight."

Maria left to pick up Michaela and Jaden and they headed back to the school.

"We would like to welcome each of you to our first ever talent competition. First we have Michael Magisto singing a song called "Around the World," he wrote himself."

The students whistled and clapped when Michael got on stage.

Then, Ms. Waters got up on stage and announced Raul and Rosita who sang a duet in Spanish. Every Spanish speaking student gave them a standing ovation. The rest of the students were looking around with a perplexed look of not understanding the words, but they clapped and cheered anyway.

"I am now announcing the group from Ms. Maria's class who have a video they want to play."

Laquisha walked up to Ms. Waters, grabbed the microphone and said, "We are going to perform this video live and we would like to dedicate this performance to Ms. Maria who believed in us and tonight we want to say we believe in her too."

"Ok, Ms. Laquisha."

Love shot over and pierced Maria's heart as Jaden climbed on her lap. Michaela glanced at tears rolling down the side of her Mom's red nose.

Darkness, aside from a few gray black lights surrounded the Gym. A few loud booms, resembling gun shots had everyone studying the crowd. Red and blue strobe lights danced above everyone in the bleachers and loud screeching sirens commanded everyone's attention. Sirens went off commanding the audience's attention. The kids began taking turns rapping their stories of drive by shootings, seeing people die on the street, young children caught in the line of fire, and robberies.

Silence filled the gym for a moment and Phillip made his way out on the stage in a blue blinging suit rapping.

"Anger pouring through our crying souls

Hearts guarded by deep hurts and pain

It begins to take it's toll…"

Feelin insane"

After the song, Maria's class captured the hearts and souls of everyone. Every single student stood up and clapped."

The kids finished their performance and waited to hear the results of the winners.

And the 3rd place winner is…Raul and Rosita!

The 2nd place winner is Michael Magisto!

And finally…The first place grand prize winner is Mrs. Maria's class!

Everyone cheered and the kids got up on stage to receive their trophy.

Phillip called Maria up on stage.

"Ms. Maria, we will miss you and this trophy belongs to you."

"I did nothing, Phillip!"

"You believed in us, Ms. Maria! You believed in us and now for the dance you owe us."

"Ms. Waters, play the rap song!"

The music in the gym got loud and Ms. Maria's class began to dance and had the whole gym dancing. Maria was unbelievably touched as she humbly accepted the trophy, saying, "I will take this with me and think of you all so often."

"Wow, Mom, they really love you."

"I love them and you too, but we have to get home to pack and be with papaw, Michaela. He really needs us right now."

The drive down south passed by like a turtle crossing a busy intersection."

"Hey Dad, how are you doing?"

"Ok, Maria. As good as any man can be after saying goodbye to the love of his life."

"I know Dad, it is hard. We should be there in about 5 hours. Do you have an appointment with the funeral home yet?"

"Yes, we need to be there at 9am tomorrow, Maria."

"Ok, Dad, will stay with you a little while if that is ok?

"Sure babe, you know you can stay with us, I mean me, anytime."

Maria and her dad walked into the lifeless room of goodbye and reality blew them both wide awake. Maria felt like she had drifted off into yesterday and was not aware of what was being spoken and her dad seemed to be in the same place.

"So tell me about Elena. What did she like to do?" Asked the Funeral Director.

Maria's dad looked at her to give the answer.

She was a teacher much of her life and retired from teaching In her early 50s. She had a passion for playing the piano and spent much of her free time feeding people at the homeless shelter. She was always a family woman."

"She sounds like a great woman, Maria. Tell me what made her human."

"She was prideful, hard on herself, did not rest enough."

So, I know you want your mom's burial, wake and funeral to be as beautiful as she is...So your total cost will be $5000."

"$5000? Can we go a little less expensive? My mom would not care how beautiful her casket is."

"Sure, Maria."

"I'm sure it's easy to make a sale when people are mourning their loved ones, Mr. Moore."

"Maria, relax."

"Sorry, Dad."

"We will have her ready by 2pm tomorrow."

"Gosh, make her sound like property," thought Maria," She was the woman I aspired to my whole life who took me to homeless shelters during Thanksgiving, played "Swans on the Lake," so lovingly and peacefully, and played with my hair when I was a little girl.

Reminding her of Michael, A hole broke open big enough for her to remember a blurr of countless and loving people walk into and out of the celebration of her husband's life. And as they made their way to the casket to say their final goodbye to Elena, she heard Michael say, "You have to start letting go, babe, we will both always be in your heart."

Maria felt the all too familiar lump in her tightening throat as she broke down in the chair next to her where she was met by Michaela and Jaden's embrace.

As the days passed by, hope began to fade. Maria found herself paralyzed to her bed, pushing herself out when she had to. She began to feel the finances start to weigh heavily on her. Michael always handled them and she was finding that things were getting more challenging since she moved back home without a job. She never asked for help from anybody and this is a time that she was going to have to ask for help. "Baby, this is the first time I have ever had to get help and you know how I have been my whole life. Can you help me out here?"

"Baby, everything will be ok, sometimes you have to ask for help to get through the bad things that happen in life. That is what people are there for." Whispered Michael.

"Yes baby, but you know how embarrassed and humiliated I am."

Maria went to the grocery store with her temporary food card and her beet red face was steaming as she noticed Maggie Murphy. Maggie was the busy body in town with a voice that spoke much more then the facts about everyone.

Maggie caught her eyes with a mischievous curiosity.

The cashier finished ringing her up and she ran out of the grocery store as quickly as she possibly could.

Maria answered her phone.

"Well, how have you been young lady?"

"I have been good, Gil. We just moved back from Chicago a few weeks ago."

"Well I'll be! Glad you came back! How have Michaela and Jaden been?"

"They have been thru so much, Gil, with losing their dad, their grandma and moving. It has been been a nightmare! How have you been?"

I have been taking it a day at a time since my wife passed away. Would you like to take an adventurous drive with me to see where she is buried?"

"Sure,Gil. What does adventurous mean?"

"Do something fun and new Gal!"

Gorgeous rolling green hills were swallowing the windy, gravel road Gil drove up. Up on one of them was a small brick home with the backdrop of a forest behind.

"Is this where you live, Gil?"

"Yes, gal, but we aren't staying here."

Gil drove Maria to an old gray barn where he got his gator out. He drove her to a distant field overflowing with wild flowers. There was a little gated garden with a sign that read "Rachel's Secret Garden." There lay a plot for both Gil and Rachel. Rachel's read "Loving mother and wife." Flowers surrounded her head stone.

"Wow, Gil, look at all those flowers surrounding her?"

"You betcha gal! Every morning for 60 years, we walked up this hill and I would pick her a flower and remind her of our first date. I haven't stopped picking her flowers. This land was owned by my parents that many years ago. On our first date I brought her here, we took a walk, I snuck a kiss, picked a flower and put it in her hair. Then I convinced her to jump in my boat and go fishing with me."

"Ahhh, so you bribed her to get her to go fishing. I see how it is."

"Of course, Gal, love is give and take you know?"

"You are funny Gil! How are you holding up without her?"

Tears began to roll down Gil's wrinkled, red Santa like cheeks.

"I'm thankful to be alive, to have my children and my grandchildren, but when that day comes that I can see her face again, joy will fill that hole in my heart."

"I understand. I feel the same about Michael and my Momma Gil. What do you miss most about her Gil?"

"I miss little things, like when she forgot her glasses but they were on her head, lost her debit card every couple of months or when she would fix my tie."

"What about you, Maria? Are there things you miss about Michael?"

"Sure. I miss watching him wrestle around with the kids while I was cooking dinner. Ive always enjoyed people watching, especially my family. We have always been more entertaining then TV."

"How are the kids doing?"

"Good. I am trying to be there more for them."

"With everything you have been through, Id imagine it can be hard. Do you have a good support system?"

"Yes, I have my dad right now, which reminds me, I have got to get home and make dinner for dad. Can we hang out in a few days? Tomorrow?"

"Tomorrow is awesome, gal!"

Maria drove to the house she grew up in and the familiar aroma of pipesmoke met her as she stepped out her door.

"Whatcha doing dad?"

"Thinking about your mom."

"I miss her too dad. What are you hungry for tonight?"

"I am not hungry babe, you just fix what you and the kids want to eat."

"You gotta eat dad."

"I know, I just can't make myself babe."

"Michaaaaaaela, Jaaaaaayden... What do you want to eat?"

"If you are cooking, nothing."

"Well, that was rude Michaela!"

"Just meant to sound just like you Mom!"

"Woooow! You can march out of this room!"

"Gladly moooooother!"

Michaela stormed to the bathroom. Maria could hear her crying. When she stormed out and up the stairs, Maria walked in and saw the family picture with those 4 letters etched in the glass. Maria broke down.

She held their picture close to her heart.

The next day, Maria called Gil to see if he wanted to hang out.

"Hey, Gal, how are you doing?"

"Doing ok."

"Why don't you hop on and we will take a little ride."

On Gil's four wheeler, they rode up a hill and across an old abandoned trail. Tall trees lined up in a formation shaded their bumpy ride in the tall grass. They finally reached a clearing with water pouring over a rock cliff. Gil stood on a tree stump and pulled out a sack lunch with sandwiches for both of them. "You hungry Gal?"

"Yes!" Exclaimed Maria

They made their way to a large tree trunk that was off to the side.

"Look over there, Gal!"

About 10 feet away was a fawn snacking. They watched for awhile before the fawn got scared and made it's way back into the woods.

"When was the last time you stood underneath a waterfall?"

"Never, Gil, it will ruin my hair"

"More the reason to do it then!"

Maria's grin reached from the waterfall to the cozy cave.

"Why are you stalling, Gal?"

"I bet it's cold! She screamed!"

Maria took her sandals off, her rainbow sundress completely drenched in water.

"This is how you waltz under a waterfall, Gal!"

He took off his fishing hat, filled it with water, and Maria's straight hair turned into ringlet curls. Gil grabbed Maria's hand and they began to dance. Her laugh echoed into the cave and through many acres of woods. At the finality of their dance, they walked over to a rock cave where Gil lit a hot fire for them to keep warm.

"Did you ever dance like this with your wife?"

"I tried a few times, but towards the end, she did not want to do anything or even eat. I didn't understand it all. She had so much to live for, her children, her grandchildren, me. I just wanted her to fight for her life and be happy. I didn't know how to help her and it made me sad that nothing I did anymore made her smile. I just wanted to see her smile one more time."

"I understand her sadness, and have been there, Gil... Well, I am there now. What do you think made her so unhappy?"

"I think the fact she had cancer just took a toll on her. She was tired of all the chemotherapy, all the pain and suffering. I don't think she died from the cancer, I honestly think she died from a broken heart."

"So sorry, Gil., I can't imagine how you feel. I know how hard it can be to get through the blues when you've been through something traumatic. I'm sure she loved you so much and just had a hard time coming out of herself to meet you."

"I know she loved me and I still get mad at her that she didn't fight harder but I'd imagine that I will feel that way for a little while."

"Tell me how you met her."

"So I walked into the fifties Diner one night. There was this beautiful woman with dark brown ringlets of long curls much like yours carrying a tray that she dropped as her eyes came to meet mine. A full plate of spaghetti and two drinks landed on my shoes. She was always so clumsy. I miss that. Her bright crystal blue eyes met mine and love exchanged forever. She smiled with her ruby red lips, and then I smiled. I flirted with her and asked for her number. She acted like she did not want to give it to me. I met her dad and mom and we were together from that moment on. Her parents loved me. I only remember one time they got mad at me. It was when they caught us kissing in the moonlight after I snuck her out of her bedroom window.

"Would you like to go for a ride on the gator, Gal?"

"Where are we going?"

"It's a surprise, out in the country, across the way a little ways, through the woods, across a valley and up some hills."

"Ummmmmm.....Should I bring a snack?"

"Don't you have a snacks hidden away in your car somewhere?"

"Are you making fun of me? I always carry peanut butter crackers with me in case my sugar bottoms out."

The ride through the many hills of wild flowers took Maria's breath away. They finally made it to a red and grey barn similar to the one close to Gil's house.

"I love old barns, Gil."

Maria snapped a picture of it.

"What are we doing here, Gil?"

"Why do you ask so many questions? Gal, come inside."

Gil climbed up the broken wooden ladder, contently sitting on top of the loft.

Maria looked at him with a look of terror for a moment.

"Well, are you going to come up here, Gal?"

"Ugh, no?"

"Maria, you know I'm 50 years older than you and I got up here pretty easy."

"Yes, Gil….Sooo!"

"You know young lady, sometimes you seem afraid to take chances, of living life."

"I'm not afraid of living life, Gil."

"Well prove it!"

"I have to say this is the first time I have ever felt pressured by an 86 year old man to climb up an old broken ladder."

"Well, there's a first for everything, and every single thing you do in life is a risk."

Maria climbed up the long ladder to the loft where Gil began reminiscing about Elena.

"The last date before we got engaged, we gazed at the stars and then we rode to this barn. It is where I got on both knees and said "Rachel Donise, will you marry me?

"On both knees, Gil?"

"Yeah, Gal, I was trying to be a little less traditional!"

"You are funny, Gil."

Right here it says "Gil plus Rachel, love is forever."

"Oh, how romantic. These things never happen anymore. I bet she wants you to know that she is happy, and that she is always in your heart."

"Thank you, Maria that means a lot!"

"Your welcome! You know Gil, over the years you become so much like the people you love. I used to joke around a lot and say, "hi, I'm Maria and Michael, glad to meet you. She's always in your heart Gil."

"I know, Gal. I know."

"So how did you and Michael meet?"

"Do you really want to know? It might be quite a bit different since it was many years after you and Rachel met"

"Thanks for the reminder of how old I am, but you know, Maria, older people and younger people have so much they can offer one another in their differences."

"True Gil...So there I was reading at the bookstore and in walks this handsome man smiling from ear to ear and a strong confidence about him, well, so I thought. He had brown curly black hair, layed his laptop down and sits at the table across from me. As I'm grading my papers and enjoying my vanilla latte he begins to talk to me. I'm in my focus mode, spill my coffee on the papers and get annoyed because I'm trying to get my papers graded so I can get home and relax. I sense this youthful spirit inside him crying out for my attention. He makes small talk, asks for my number. I gave it to him, thinking I probably did not have time for dating even if he did call me, yet my heart kept saying he would one day call me. I waited a week and thought my heart must have been wrong. Then he called and asked me to go out on a date. I unintentionally pushed him away at first but he was very persistent. He was different than every guy I've ever dated, very easy to trust. I realized that I would probably never find a person as committed as he was and so we dated a year, got engaged for 2 years and finally got married. Shortly after that we had Michaela and Jaden came 10 years later."

"You can't always know the difference between whether anyone is lying and telling the truth. Why spend the limited days you have on this earth, trying to find the lie in something. How joyful would that be? Rachel would ask me questions from time to time, get concerned whenever I talked to a woman. The funny thing about that is since she has been gone, not one lady has stolen my heart, well, besides you, but you don't count."

"Gee thanks, Gil!"

"Well, you're too young for me. She never saw how much I loved her because she was too busy focusing on fixing her imperfections. I really loved her and she is the one and only love of my life. Spending so much time worrying about whether somebody is going to hurt you is never a good thing."

"How do you prevent that from happening, Gil?"

"You can't, but what you can do is trust God and think before approaching a situation where you might get wronged, lied to or cheated on. You will drive yourself mad and crazy if you are afraid all the time, Gal."

"I am just living life and I don't worry if it will happen again. I do get scared alot that Damien will come follow through on his threats."

"What do you have that you can claim still as your own, Gal?"

"Well, I have my beautiful kids...my self-respect, love in my heart and beautiful memories."

"Exactly, and no one's going to steal your heart and your soul. Everything else can always be restored and you will always have me as a friend." Laughed Gil.

The following day, Gil and Maria met at the local diner to grab a few steaks

"Hey Gil!"

They both hugged.

"Whatcha hungry for. Gal?"

"Of course, my favorite again, steak and a sweet potato smothered in brown sugar and butter. Yumm, Gil!"

"Dinner is on me, Gal."

"How sweet, Gil, thank you!"

"What's new today, Gal?"

"Everything has been good, aside for Jaden has been asking about his Daddy all the time and Michaela spouted off something hateful. I think she misses her Daddy too."

"Do you have any male friends you can talk to, to take him out fishing, play basketball, ride the four wheeler?"

"Well, I can do that, Gil."

"I know you can do it Gal, but he needs that male bonding too. I don't mind to take him fishin'."

"That is very sweet of you Gil!"

They finished their lunch and Maria went home.

"Jaden, what do you think about us finding someone you can go out fishing with like an older guy pal?"

"Sounds fun, I would really like to do some boy stuff. I really miss Daddy, but if I can't do anything with Daddy I would like to do a few guy only things mom. Guy time is really important to me."

Maria thought to herself, "how blessed am I?"

"Am I not a tomboy enough for you Jaden?" Maria laughed.

"Of course you're enough for me, Mommy, I love you, but it is nice to hang out with guys too!" Remember when me and Daddy used to go to the games together? I miss that so much. I miss that guy time and we would get ice cream and talk about leaving you and Michaela alone. He would talk about us going to the lake house by ourselves and fishing because you guys get a little moody sometimes. We talked a lot about stuff."

"What other things did he say, Jaden?"

"Just that he would keep my dreams safe, Mommy."

"Would you like to share some of those dreams, Jaden?"

"Maybe one day, Mommy but right now they make me feel very special, like he is still in my heart."

"I understand that, Buddy and you will always feel him in your heart. Did you hear that? If you listen quietly, you can hear him whisper. I'm not trying to get anybody to take the place of your Daddy. I just thought it would be nice for you to meet somebody that's a guy cuz you know me and your sister are women and sometimes hard to understand."

"Yes, thank you Mommy, I love you! Will you read a story to me?"

"You know, I have read you 3 books today already, but of course I will read you another one Jaden, I love you! How about we go out on the hammock?"

"Alright Mommy!"

10

Life's heartaches had begun to finally take it's toll on Maria's once lively spirit. She began to feel like a gigantic hummer had wrecklessly and repeatedly driven over her tattered, fragile heart to the point it was barely recognizeable. She realized the time had come to begin acknowledging the pieces she was responsible for and the decisions she made. Just a step or two away from her purpose had her taking a bite out of the temptation to run away from dealing with her heart breaks.

A recurrent story played through her mind of a woman frequently hurting over and over again. Maria noticed her mom's bible sitting on the octagon shaped cedar wood coffee table. She grabbed it and went outside on the deck to relax. Out popped a highlighted and underlined verse.

Every man according as he purposeth in his heart, so let him give; not grudgingly, or of necessity: for God loveth a cheerful giver

She was wiped out, tired of putting herself out there and tempted to throw in the towel when life kept handing her disappointments. She knew that giving love was Gods greatest purpose for her life. She saw a vision of Jesus being persecuted and beaten with blood streaming down his face and realized all that he went through so she could experience God's grace.

God whispered, "I will guide you if you listen more closely to my voice. My will for you is to be around people who cherish you and your loving heart."

"Where have you been, God and why have I not felt your spirit?"

"I have been here this whole time carrying you my love and the real test of faith is when you can't feel me."

Maria called Gil.

"Would you like to go for a walk, Gil?"

"Not sure I can, Gal."

"How come Gil?"

"Got some stuff to take care of today, but I will call you later."

Maria began to feel even more sadness, wondering what she did to deserve Gil not coming to hang out with her. He had become her best friend.

Maria answered her phone.

"Hi Gil, can you come out now?"

"Sure, Gal, I will meet you at the park we first met in an hour?"

"Sounds good Gil!"

They stood and talked for a few lightening speed moments before walking the trail and found their way to the large log Maria once struggled to climb over.

"You see that over there?"

"What Gil?"

That butterfly reminds me of you, Gal!"

"Howso, Gil?"

"It once was settled ever so comfortably in it's warm fuzzy cocoon before it began the journey through many changes. With each change was a struggle but one day, it finally transformed into a beautiful butterfly. It looks like it's wing is broken like yours was when you came home from Up North. And it just needs a little time and tenderness before it can fly again. You remind me a lot of that butterfly. You've grown so much, Gal. After you first came back from Chicago, you were grieving. You are doing things to help other people and you're so strong."

"Gil, you are lifting me up so often, but there are days I still wake up and feel like a truck has run me over. Thank you for noticing, though. That is so sweet."

"You know Gal, if you were twenty years younger, I'd sweep you off your feet."

"Yeah, yeah, yeah, Gil you told me this before."

"Gil, you know, you are one of the wisest guys I've ever met and I so appreciate you and am very grateful that we met."

"I'm grateful for you too, Doll."

"Maria began to think about What Gil said and joy filled her heart as she began to believe in herself and her transformation.

11

Though Maria had made some decisions which had thrown her into the fire of fear, doubt and insecurity, she saw beautiful things birth from leaping off high cliffs into lifes uncertainties. She gained strength, a stronger faith, more love within herself. Her whole being was inside an unfamiliar world with very few things to hold onto for safety.

There were good parts to the familiar, but she knew that it was time to start a new chapter. She had no idea what her next step was. Each day she began to take a step away from familiar. Every step created a challenge. Every challenge built her strength. Doubts, fears and insecurity still swam around, but dreams, fun, rest, love, they were the big fish, and they began to swallow her doubts and fears.

As Maria was listening to the news she heard the local bank had been robbed. The men drove away in a black SUV. Maria remembered Damien reading a book about robberies and he had a black SUV. She remembered the time she borrowed his phone and saw that he had left an article up on how to rob a bank and get away with it. She knew if she questioned him about it, he would just call her crazy like he did every time he was sitting on the chair of accountability. There were so many different layers and facets to Damien and there was a mysterious side she was never able to reach. He was intentional in all that he did with a childlike vulnerability. Thoughts, facts and fears were flying around her mind with all of the craziness. There seemed to be no order for awhile. One day, the fuzzy picture cleared up and Maria became body slammed by some true facts. As she pieced the facts together and grew stronger, she began to trust her instincts and was ready to pursue it farther. She remembered in Michael's email the case of the missing woman. She was robbed at gunpoint and that there was a black SUV involved. Then she remembered seeing a shadow in Damien's attic room. He had talked about being in prison for a robbery.

Maria called the police department and for some reason the number just kept ringing. It seemed like every time she tried to fix something, she would collide with roadblocks. She decided it would be best to head there on her own. The drive seemed to take decades. When she finally arrived and began to tell her story, she was interrupted by an officer who drowned her voice with his own. He told her to write it all down and they would call her if they needed anything. Maria began contemplating her own sanity. "At least it is out of my hands." She thought.

Maria and the kids made their way to Gil's to play in nature, got the 4 wheeler out and road down to the pond. It had frozen over thick enough to go ice skating, but Maria was afraid they still might cut through, so they just stood and looked at the beautiful view with tree of icicles behind it.

She remembered one time when her and Michael went ice skating down there. He brought out the courage in her. Although skating on a pond was not as smooth as the rink, it still made her feel like she was dancing with the wind in a whole new world of beauty. The dripping icicles from the trees caught her eyes.

They built a fire in the pit and sat with the warmth for a bit.

"Mommy, do you miss Daddy?"

"Sure Jaden, there are times I miss your Daddy, but hes in my heart and hes always in your heart."

"Michaela, did you just fart?"

"No, Jaden, did you?"

"Nope, wanna play a game?"

"Sure, how about tag? You are it!"

Maria could barely see above the wall between hers and Michaelas heart. And finally one day, the wall exploded with hurt as skating on the surface of her mothers heart turned into cutting it deeper.

"You are right, Michaela...Mommy did not know how to heal the emptiness and should have reached harder for God. I wasted too much time and I am so sorry for that."

Tears streamed down both of their faces as God filled the emptiness in both of their hearts.

The only thing I know to do is to build a new life with you each day, love you and your brother the rest of our lives and the few years I have left before you go off to college. Ive been so angry with all this pain and Mommy became very depressed. One day, when you stop being angry with who I was, I hope you will love who I am becoming. I love you no matter what and hope you know this."

"I know you love me, Mom."

They hugged.

Maria's phone rang.

"Hey Angelia!"

"Hey sweetheart! What's going on?"

"Just had a heart to heart with Michaela. What's new with you? It has been quite awhile since we last talked. How have you and Brody been?"

"Brody and I are staying together."

"What...What made you decide to stay together?"

"You know, the idea of being in a relationship with that woman sent the wrong feelings up my spine. Then one day Brody took me to the park and we rolled down the hills like we did when we were kids. I fell in love with him all over again."

"So you are bi?"

"You know, I read one day that everyone has a part of them that can be attracted to the same sex."

"Interesting perspective, Angelia."

"I would prefer to instead be called a woman fighting a battle of temptations every day like everyone else."

"Sounds like an accurate assessment."

"You know what Maria? I decided that the 20 years of marriage was worth the battle."

"I am so glad you guys worked it out sweetie."

"Thank you, Maria."

12

The next morning came as quickly as time passed whenever her summer vacation had come and went. Maria continued to have moments of battling the boxing match between waking up and staying in bed. Every once in awhile her mind would roll her eyes at habitually happy morning people. This day happened to be very different then the rest. She saw a ray of light shining a path from her heart and out the door of her dark cozy bedroom. She wondered if she was dreaming and then a revelation hit her that she had become acquainted with her dream.

A few touches of uneasiness but excitement for the uncertainty awaiting dashed into her mind. She was so comfy under the covers and rather then following the light outside the door, she thought she would snooze a little longer before her eyes would finally open to the rays tickling her nose.

"What did I miss when I snoozed, God?"

"You haven't missed a thing baby doll. I was revealing your dreams to you."

For a few moments Maria felt shame as she pondered her rebellion to God. She had not seen his light in what seemed like a decade. Her mind traveled back to the past. How many times had her busy, preoccupied and worrying mind wandered from the many songs and cries of her heart and soul. The hands of the clock had finally slowed down enough for her heart and mind to finish what the other started.

Maria went to pick up Jaden's medicine from the pharmacy and ran into Renae, a well respected and prominent woman in her community.

"How have you been, Renae?"

"I have been good, Maria."

"How is Mr. Jones, doing?"

"I don't know, honey, we divorced shortly after this happened."

Renae pointed to a long scar on her neck

"What happened, Ranae?"

"I hated my life, hated my husband and he kept threatening he would ruin me if I left. So, one day, I decided to take control of my own life, take some pills and hang myself."

"I hope that does not make you think badly of me, Maria."

"No, Renae, I am thinking how strong you are for sharing this. How did you live through it Renae?"

"Well, the rope broke and I fell a few feet."

"My ex husband, that jerk, came upstairs and screamed at me about the blood on the carpet. The rope had cut my neck!"

"My son who was 15 came upstairs and called 911."

"I am so glad you lived through everything, Renae."

"Are you happy now?"

"Yes, I live in a house the quarter of the mansion I used to live in, but my new husband and I have so much fun together. We go on many adventures and he rarely gets angry."

"Awesome, Renae, How did you get through all that?"

I prayed every day for healing, got a counselor and little by little, day by day, God finally delivered me from it."

"Your story has really reached my heart, Renae."

Maria left thinking about how hearing Renaes story had made her feel less alone and it inspired her to open up to more people. She wondered when another life lesson might appear and when she would get another opportunity to gain a new nugget of wisdom.

The next day, Maria encountered a cute couple with a striking resemblance to one another sitting on a wooden bench in the park...She so sweetly adjusted his collar. He gazed into her eyes as she talked.

"Hi, young lady!"

"Hi……..you guys seem to be so in love."

"We are. Our love has been seasoned with so many different facets of life experiences, struggles and blessings."

Maria began dreaming about swinging on a porch swing with her grand children on one side and her soulmate on the other.

"How long have you been married if you don't mind me asking."

"60 years to this beautiful lady, young lady." Said the man.

"Wow, what contributed to you being married for so long?"

"Its alot of compromise." Said the woman.

Maria thought to herself, "well, that's not rocket science."

Then, she looked into his eyes and saw one tiny tear begin its journey down his wrinkles and the color of his face was the color of his heart. His feelings for her were out in the open, yet it was one of the rarest things Maria had seen.

"Not one thing in life is perfect, not him or I. You just have to do good with what you've got sweetie." Said the woman.

"We spend all of our lives looking for perfect, only to find that perfect isnt real. Love is real. And love is found mostly in imperfect places." Said the man.

Maria went back and met the kids.

"How about a picnic at the lake?"

"Yeah, Mom!"

"Mooom, Jaden. No more Mommy?"

"Getting too big for Mommy, Mom."

"How are you guys doing?"

"Fine, Mom."

"You don't sound ok, Michaela."

"You don't care anyway Mom."

"That is not true, I love you and want to know what is going on."

"Well, you have seem distracted, Mom."

"You are right, I have been. I am going to see a grief counselor. I am so sorry I have been so inside myself."

"Good. I forgive you, Mom. We have been worried about you."

"I don't want you guys to worry about me. I worry about you."

The next day, the noises that frequently fought for Maria's attention had silenced. When she walked outside on this particular day, she heard the birds sing a brand new song. It reminded her of the times she went to the lakehouse camping with her parents. They traveled there almost every weekend until Maria was a teenager. They arrived on a Friday night, her dad would grab some matches and lighter fluid and they gathered wood together. They would roast brats and made pies with a couple of pieces of bread and cherries. Her favorite was the gooey, messy chocolate roasted marshmallow and graham cracker treat. They would swing on the swing watching the sky change to different colors as the bright sun gradually disappeared out of sight. That began their gazing at the brightly shining miniature created stars adorning many of the trees. The cries of coyotes, ribits of frogs and crickets sang them many touching songs of freedom.

Some mornings they would wake right before the sun came alive, to the birds singing the sweetest songs. They took walks around the lake and repeatedly jumped off the dock her dad built, feeling splashes of water cool their hot dark tanned bodies. Every once in awhile her dad would take her floating around on the air mattress. The sun rays turned her face and nose red.

After burning all that energy, they built bottomless appetites for baked ziti and let the air vents cool them off before drifting off into their traditional midday "eye rest" breaks.

Around mid afternoon Maria's mom would grab 15 minutes of silence by sending them on a walk around the lake with their dad. Maria wondered what her mom did during those times and stayed back one day to catch her sneaking a bite of chocolate and dancing to Frank Sinatra tunes. Her mom well earned her quiet time with all the juggling she did and sacrifices she made to ensure her family never stopped laughing.

Maria and her mom had their moments and especially when their menstrual cycles were almost exactly the same. In fact, you could bet at that time it was best for them both to sit in separate cages roaring at the passerbys waiting for the thick hormones to free them back into the wild. Maria's dad, always hanging close to heaven, learned how to keep that cycle of their month very calm and peaceful. He kept chocolate in his bedroom inside his top drawer and anytime thing's got rough, he would go into the bedroom, eat a piece and enjoy his peace and quiet. Every once in awhile he might gently throw a piece to them, as he pictured his hand being eaten off and would run into the yard to do some yard work. He was such a patient and understanding man.

A few months of staying with her dad had María ready to move back to the old house. She began to go through everything in the attic and saw the crib that Jaden and Michaela both slept in as babies. It was a sleigh bed made of dark wood with very few knicks on it.. It looked almost brand new and was 13 years old. Getting rid of it did not feel right. She decided she would try her hand at creating a desk, she saw for Jaden out of it. Getting it out of the attic meant taking it apart piece by piece with an Allen Wrench, but in a couple hours she had it up and ready.

It looked really adorable in the living room with her furniture and her own creation made it feel really homey. The only thing missing was a board so Jaden could write on it. Throughout the day, Ariel would periodically get up on the board and lay there. Maria began to see it as a glamorous cat bed vs a kid desk. As Maria glanced at Ariel she wondered if in all the distractions she missed that Ariel was pregnant, or if it was just her wild and crazy imagination. For a brief moment she thought about how proud Michael would have been seeing her put that together by herself.

The next day, Maria came home and heard a high pitched noise coming from her bedroom. As she walked back there a single "meuu" sounded like a couple of "meuu's" coming from her dresser.

There was one drawer open with Marias bath towel draped over. Maria left the room to start a load of laundry and popped back in to see Ariel's head popping out of the drawer. When she opened the other drawer she found , a tiger striped girl and an orange boy.

"Michaela, Jaden come here!"

"What, Mommy?"

Jaden was running down the hallway to Maris's room.

"Ariel had babies? Did you know she was gonna have babies Mommy?"

"Yep, and unfortunately, I did not know she was having babies."

"Can I hold one. Can we keep em?"

"Yes and we will see on keeping them."

"What's going on? Omg, how did that happen?" Asked Michaela.

Well, remember that day that Ariel got outside and we had to scare that stray away from her?"

"Yes, Mom."

"Well, one of the kittens looks a lot like her."

Maria thought a lot about what was to be discovered of this new adventure and all the worries she had.   There lay a momma, just like her with a couple of kittens . Ariel's nurturing her kittens brought an unexpected healing to Michaela, Jaden and Maria.

Maria ran to the path she and Gil first met and noticed something different this time. Where once she saw green grass of the summer, the dew of the Spring, the orange leaves of the fall and the snowfall in the wintertime, she saw flowers blooming of all sorts and there was a hidden path she had not ever seen before. She made her way on that path and encountered more and more tree limbs to climb over.

Maria answered her phone.

"What are you doing, Gal?"

"I am running at that place we met and thinking about how busy you have been lately."

"I have missed you, Gal."

"I have missed you too, Gil."

"How about an adventure, Gal?"

"Sounds like fun, Gil. Are you coming to pick me up?"

"Yes. Does Jaden and Michaela want to come too?"

"Michaela is out with her friends, so I will bring Jaden.

"I'll meet you at your house in an hour."

Gil arrived and took them on an hour long drive to a house hidden away in the country.

"Knock, knock!"

Gil walked into the mostly wooded interior of the back of the house where the aroma of coffee gently filled the air.

"Hello," said a woman dressed in scrubs faintly from another room. She is resting."

Maria, Gil and Jaden walked into the sun room where there was classical music playing and the view of a large lake out the bay windows. The cardinals danced to the rhythm of the mingling chimes playing in the background. The hospital bed in the middle of the room, with a skinny, wrinkled aged woman laying in it, shook Maria's heart awake.

"How are you doing Ms. Rose?" Asked Gil.

"Ok," muttered Rose in a very solemn tone.

"What's your pain on a scale of 1-10 Rose?"

"About a 4, Gil, my pain medicine is kicking in."

"Come here Maria and Jaden, meet Rose."

As Maria walked over to say "Hi," horror and fear covered Rose's face.

Maria grasped her hand with enough firmness that Rose could feel Maria's love transcend to her heart. Instantly, Rose's eyebrows relaxed from the "on guard" position and her face glowed peacefully.

"How do you guys know each other?" Asked Maria.

"My wife and Rose have known each other since they were babies. I have been coming to visit Rose every day since hospice came in a few weeks ago."

Maria looked at Gil and thought to herself "did I really make a comment about Gil not coming around? He has been spending time taking care of his friend."

Maria knew the blessing of their friendship was truly hers.

"Would you like to see some old pics of my wife and Rose, Maria?"

"Sure, Gil."

"This is when they were in their early 20s, Gal."

"What are you guys doing in that pic?"

"We had just walked around a cemetary at midnight and the ladies thought it would be fun to sit the back of the truck.

They screamed every time mud flew in the back and hit them. Good times!"

Maria saw two beautiful women, one blond and one burnette which reminded her of the unforgettable times she had with Angelia.

"What about this one, Gil?"

"You know that game people play now, where the driver and the passenger get out and switch seats at a stop sign?"

"Chinese Fire Drills?"

"Yes, the ladies thought that game would be fun, but did not know you had to put the car in park."

"Oh no, Gil."

"The car started to speed up toward a lake. Rose saved the day."

Gil looked at her with a smile.

"How did she save it?"

She dove her upper body into the bottom of the car and pushed the brake, seconds before they would have crossed over into a pond behind a nursing home with teenagers skinnydipping.

"What about this one?"

"It was when we all went to Cozumel. We sat on the beach drinking margaritas til the sun rose and I captured a photograph of my wife's profile. She looked so beautiful, the way she glistened in the sunlight. I just loved seeing her in her sunhat and flower sundress. Then a few men picked both the ladies up and spinned them around a few times...Some kind of good luck dance they do in Cozumel."

Rose smiled graciously as Gil told her he would be back in the morning.

Maria was uncertain what to say.

"I love you, Rose." Maria said.

"I love you too, Maria." Said Rose.

As they walked to the car, Jaden spoke up, "Mommy, that woman is the most beautiful woman."

Maria looked at Jaden and smiled. She knew he had taken a walk inside her soul and discovered her inner beauty.

"Gil, what a wonderful adventure, but I am so sorry about your friend."

"At my age Gal, it happens more and more. Going to see her reminds me of my wife,"

"They both looked so beautiful and full of life, Gil.

"They both were, Gal."

"You are such a special person, Gil."

"So are you, Maria. So are you, Jaden."

"Thank you Gil!" Said Jaden.

"How about something to eat, guys?"

"Sure, Gil!"

"Are you hungry Jaden?"

"Yes, of course, Gil."

"What are you hungry for, Buddy?"

"Do you like fried catfish, Gal?"

"It's been awhile, but that sounds good!"

They made their way to a restaurant on the river.

"Have you been here before Gal?"

"I can't say I have, Gil."

They enjoyed dinner and made their way to a ferry.

"Would you like to get out of the car guys?"

"We can get out?"

"Absolutely, Jaden!"

"Everything ok, Gal?"

"Yeah, just thinking about Michael."

As time passed rather quickly, they headed back home to meet Michaela patiently waiting for them.

"Where have you been?"

"We went to visit one of Gil's friends.

"It took you long enough, Mom!"

"She was beautiful, Michaela." Said Jaden.

"She was also dying." Said Maria.

Michaela got really quiet as Maria approached her and hugged her.

"I know it hasn't been easy since your dad died, but I want you to know how much I love you both so, so much.

"I love you too mom, but I am ready to enjoy life again."

"I hear you, Michaela."

"Besides, it's been all about you and your feelings. What about mine and Jaden's feelings?"

"I am sorry, Michaela."

"Sorry, that's all you have to say? We miss Daddy every single day and we need to count on you to be here for us."

"I am here for you every day."

"Your body is, but we want all of your heart and mind."

"I have ADD!"

"That's not an excuse. You could try to focus harder."

"Ok. How about I focus a little harder at…"

Maria began to chase Michaela through the house with a pillow.

"Stop Mom!" yelled Michaela grabbing Maria's phone off the desk. I am going to take a picture of you!"

"No you won't," yelled Maria as she grabbed a hold of the phone.

"Truce?" exclaimed Maria

"Mommy," said Jaden," will you come play with me?"

"Ok, Jaden, for a little while and then it is time for bed."

The sunset came to visit so quickly and Maria headed to Jaden's room to tuck him in.

"Mommy, I miss Daddy. What do you think he is doing right now?"

"I think he is dancing with angels dressed in pretty dresses in heaven," said Maria as she hugged him.

"How about some butterfly kisses and you sleep with Ernie?"

"Ernie? I have not slept with him in a very long time."

"How come?"

"Cause he has holes in his legs."

"Maybe we should throw him away?"

"Noooooo," yelled Jaden, "last time you threw him away I found him in the trash remember?"

"Yes, how about I try to fix it?"

"Sounds good Mommy."

"Mommy, will you read me that bed time story with pictures of the leaves?"

"Sure, but you know, you can probably read your own story, Buddy."

"I know, but I am too tired and just want to listen, Mom."

"Ok, sweetie."

Although Maria was really tired, she began to read the story. As she continued to thumb through, she noticed a folded up paper that looked like a book marker. She opened it up and began to read it.

Dear Maria,

As I lie here about to drift asleep, I take a moment to think about how much beauty you have brought to our marriage. Where once everything was about me, I have learned how to truly love. You have given me two children, your love and a life many men dream of having. If I died tomorrow, I would die peacefully, knowing I have lived my life completely and fully. I look into your eyes and see your old soul baring much wisdom. I feel the soft touch of your giving heart and become weak in my knees. You are powerful beyond measure. You are love and I will love you for the rest of eternity.

With great love,

Michael

"Mommy, is that a letter from Daddy?"

"Yes, yes it is, Buddy."

"Will you read it to me?"

"Sure Buddy."

Maria grabbed a hold of Jaden and cuddled with him, reading it once again and unaware of her hardness, a crack began to split open into her heart.

The morning light shone into Jaden's bedroom and Maria went out to take a walk with her cup of coffee. She held the letter from Michael close to her chest. It was as if she picked up a piece of her heart that had been lost for so long, dusted it off and sewed it back on.

He was absolutely amazing at speaking words which breathed life into her world and although life had brought her tragic and discouraging times, they were words she needed to once again hear. She often heard God speak to her through his words.

13

"So, what do you think about running a half marathon with me Michaela?"

"What, mom? You know I hate to run,"

"Come on, mother daughter bonding."

"Can't we bond eating ice cream?"

"We do that already. We can train together."

"Ok, for you mom, but this will cost you. Where?"

"Let's look some up online."

Together they looked for runs and found one in Nashville to register for.

"When do you want to start running, Michaela?"

"Tonight, mom."

A loud roar of thunder and rain began to tap dance on the rooftop.

"Guess we aren't running today, mom."

"The rain will stop sometime, but you know, since the thunder has stopped, I say we go outside and run in it."

"Mother, have you lost your mind?"

"Yes, but I found my heart. Your dad and I used to run in the rain all the time!"

Maria took Jaden to the neighbors and Maria and Michaela went for a run around the neighborhood.

"You look like you are getting tired, daughter!"

"Nope, not me, just gonna pass your slow butt up. You sure are talkative the last few weeks, Mom."

"Yes, not really sure what has happened."

"It happened shortly after you found that letter from Daddy."

"Maybe I found and reclaimed a piece of my heart I thought died when Daddy died."

"It's nice to see you smiling again, Mom. You know, Daddy will always be in our hearts."

"Of course."

"If he is living in your heart, don't you want to be happy?"

"I have never thought of it this way. Of course."

"I try to think of it like the only way Daddy can live in this life is if he can live through my heart and my experiences. Sometimes I ask him what he thinks of what I am doing and I imagine he answers me."

"That is such a beautiful way to put it. You are and will always be so special. You remind me of your Daddy in so many ways."

"Thanks mom and we could not have made it through everything without you."

The next morning came so quickly and Maria was craving some solitude, so she grabbed her running shoes and took in the beauty of the trail on the winding path in the woods behind the park.

She ran about a mile of the trail when she felt the sting of a wasp on her shoulder.

"Dang it!"

She saw a vision of herself falling to the ground, and being unconscious for days. She wondered if she should turn back, but decided to keep going.

"Omg! There are no cougars in Illinois?!"

From previous walks, Maria noticed the trees growing closer together and the ground seemed higher then ever before. She felt like she was a weightless feather effortlessly blowing across the woods.

She looked off into the distance and caught a vision of the bottoms of the woods where Michael and her used to picnic and watch the deer. She heard him whisper "Let go, baby. I am always in your heart."

Tears flowed down her cheeks. As her heart felt pierced by the aarow of loves heartbreaks, it dawned on her that the last year she had taken a walk into the abandoned pieces of her heart. Where once the doors were sealed shut by the guards of her soul, they were now swinging so effortlessly. She knew it was a walk she had to take with some painful stings but promised new discoveries, awakening memories and a greater appreciation for God's love and grace today.

She then heard crackling in the leaves and a large black and white pitbull came running toward her.

"After hearing a few stories about pitbulls killing people on the news, she was tempted to climb up onto the large rock and cower inside a small cave."

"Be still," God whispered.

She let the dog come closer and it began to lick her hand. She heard a familiar voice yell "Baaaaailey!"

"Mr.. Berndino, Peter! How have you been?"

"Good,well, aside from the accident, and riding around in this damn thing."

"What happened?"

"Motorcycle accident. You?"

"Well, life has been a bit of a challenge the last few years. As you know, Michael passed away and I have had some hard times. Then my mother passed away."

"Wow, I am so sorry, I did not know your mom passed away. How is your dad doing?"

"He is managing the best that he can. I followed him to her grave the other day and he sat there awhile talking to her. He writes her love letters every night as well. We both miss her."

"What about the teaching Up North?"

"You know...I moved home for a few reasons, but I don't regret a bit of it. I learned so much from my students and to this day, when I think of strength, I think of them. There were moments I have struggled with getting out of bed and I remember what many of them have to go through just to make it to school every day. I would say I learned much more then I taught them."

"I am sure they learned a lot from you too. How are the kids doing? I saw Michaela the other day out at the diner with what looked like a few friends."

"She is doing good. Got straight As in Chicago and is glad to be back this semester with some of her other friends. How is Jill doing?"

"Jill and I are no longer together."

"Omg, what happened?"

"One day, after my accident, she was home and we were cooking together. The next day all of her stuff was gone with a note saying thanks for 15 years of marriage but I just don't feel like being married anymore."

Then I received divorce papers at the school. Life's cruelest endeavor tore my heart up. I was choking on my tears with an audience of innocent kids staring back at me. Not too shortly after that I ran into her and her boyfriend. He was pretty buff riding his bad motorcycle but she did not seem happy nor the same."

"I am so sorry Peter. I can only imagine how that made you feel. You are such a good man."

"Thank you. It's been awhile since anyone complimented me."

"You are welcome! It is so good to see you."

"Are you still teaching these days?"

"No. Things have been pretty tough after mom passed away. I have been taking it day by day, but I am waiting to hear back about a job as a volunteer for hospice.

"What a beautiful thing to do, Maria!"

"Thank you, Peter!"

"So, would it be an acceptable thing to ask for your number?"

"Yes, you can have my number."

"What about a date?"

"You are really pushing it," Maria laughed, "But I think that sounds like a nice idea."

"I know, but you are worth it."

"Thank you, Peter. How about I push you back to your car?"

"That would make me one lucky man."

Maria walked into the house and stood in front of the mirror. For a moment, she caught a glimpse of her unproportional thighs, aging skin and thinning hair. She realized it was time to accept herself for all of who she was. She thought about her journey from losing the love of her life to moving to a different culture and losing her mother. She realized that although the why's of life drove her curiosity, the greatest anecdote to the pain in the world was the gentlest touches of unconditional love.

"Thank you, God."

And so it was her time to fly...

The beginning of a brand new chapter awaits.

In Loving Memory of:

Dorothy Irene Cabanatuan

Roberta Donise Kotschi

Barbara M Levy

Robert A Levy

Justin Levy

Keitha L Davis

Jack Simmons

Sarah Cocanour Dalton

Kristopher John Mohr

She was a lively, energetic, passionate and driven go getter until Stacey experienced "rock bottom." She left a job of 14 years, lost significant people in her family, had a miscarriage, filed for bankruptcy, suffered severe emotional abuse and filed for divorce while pregnant with her fourth son. All of this trauma, found her muddling through a thick fog of a cold and lonely depression and intense fear. For the very first time in her life, she felt worthless and did not feel like her presence added much value to the world anymore. What she learned was that there are times in life we tumble, where we all need an extra hand, but most importantly, unconditional love. She looked into the eyes of her 4 children and was determined to fight for her heart to open again, for her family's dreams and take the steps necessary to heal from the past and become the woman and mother God intended her to become. With God, her children and angels who crossed her path, she has courageously swam further then she ever has in her life.

Once being passionate about dedicating her life to inspiring others, she continues to hold on to her faith in God's purpose for her life, and her comeback story. She dreamt of the day she could be an extra hand and inspire hope to someone else.

Stacey founded Butterflies Fly, a business dedicated to inspiring the world to" Mend Your Wings and Fly." She founded Butterflies Fly 5k's to shed light and lift up charities in the community. She has spent 20 years coaching in Corporate America, 7 years coaching business owners in network marketing and has spent the last 18 months inspiring people in the creative industries. Stacey will coach you out of your comfort zone, into the ocean of vulnerability, and ask you the questions that inspire self discovery. For Life Coaching, Group Online Coaching and/or Business Coaching, 5k support or additional opportunities, email Stacey at diazstacey777@gmail.com

Made in the USA
Coppell, TX
06 December 2024